ARE YOU AN EXPERT ON ENRIQUE?

1. What are his favorite foods?
2. What is his biggest pet peeve?
3. What is his astrological sign?
4. When was his first kiss?
5. Where did he grow up?

Answers: 1. Hamburgers, hot dogs, and Cuban food.
2. Being compared to his
father; 3. Taur

St. Martin's Paperbacks Titles
by Elina and Leah Furman

Enrique Iglesias
James Van Der Beek
Lyte Funkie Ones

ENRIQUE
IGLESIAS

ELINA AND LEAH FURMAN

St. Martin's Paperbacks

NOTE: If you purchased this book without a cover you should be aware that this book is stolen property. It was reported as "unsold and destroyed" to the publisher, and neither the author nor the publisher has received any payment for this "stripped book."

ENRIQUE IGLESIAS

Copyright © 2000 by Elina and Leah Furman.
Cover photograph CORBIS Outline/Alan Silfen ©.

All rights reserved. No part of this book may be used or reproduced in any manner whatsoever without written permission except in the case of brief quotations embodied in critical articles or reviews. For information address St. Martin's Press, 175 Fifth Avenue, New York, NY 10010.

ISBN: 0-312-97523-6

Printed in the United States of America

St. Martin's Paperbacks edition / March 2000

10 9 8 7 6 5 4 3 2 1

For mom

Acknowledgments

We'd like to thank everyone who has helped bring this book to print, including our editor Glenda Howard for all her foresight, effort, and dedication, and our agent Giles Anderson for so many things that we wouldn't even know where to begin the list. As always, our mother Mira for her support and inspiration. And John Nikkah for his invaluable assistance in the research department.

We'd also like to express our gratitude to the various Enrique Iglesias fans, especially Karen Labs, whose anecdotes, photos, and enthusiasm made writing this book all the more fun. Lastly, many thanks are due to Daphne Lockyer, author of *Julio Iglesias: The Unsung Story*, for providing us with a detailed portrait of Enrique's family history, as well as his younger years.

ONE

Father of Mine

Lounging in a plush armchair and waiting patiently for the battalions of anxious reporters to finish off their now-familiar lines of inquiry, Enrique is the image of nonchalance and detachment. With his shy smile, rumpled locks, and signature black leather pants, the world's top-selling Latin artist looks as above it all as his albums' sales figures. It seems as though nothing could faze him now; nothing, except a couple of questions that would put a dark cloud over every record sale, over every fan's smiling face, and over every glance in the bathroom mirror.

"Is there any truth to the rumor that you and your father compete when it comes to record sales?"

"Do you think you would be as successful if it wasn't for your father?"

Few things affect Enrique Iglesias as deeply as the mention of his father. Forever cast into the role of the "rising son," the young singer has grown to re-sent the implication. And when you consider that everything he has achieved—the awards, the critical acclaim, the unsurpassable sales record—he has achieved on his own, it's not hard to understand why.

"I don't like to get into it but I'm tired of hearing, 'Do you think you sell more records because of your dad?'

"We're two different personalities. We're two different singers with two different styles and, most importantly, we're from two different generations."

Pointing out the obvious inconsistencies of the "like father, like son" theory cannot be easy on the Latin crooner. After all, the man he is so intent on distancing himself from is none other than his own flesh and blood, his legendary father, Julio Iglesias.

But listen closely to Enrique's words and you'll hear a wisdom that is as old as the most ancient empires, as timeless as the struggles of generations past and present, and as certain as the future of rebellious youth. To truly understand a man, it is often not enough to examine his dreams and aspirations. One must look at the whole person, and see his fears, or all that he endeavors *not* to become. Such is the case with Enrique Iglesias.

Enrique's story begins more than thirty years before his arrival into the world. While the singer might not like to dwell on the fact, his tale, like those of so many others, begins with the birth of his father. Born to a privileged Spanish family on September 23, 1943, Julio Jose Iglesias was brought kicking and screaming into this world by Julio Iglesias Puga and Rosario de la Cueva.

As one of Madrid's leading gynecologists, Julio's father presided over a posh and well-respected household. Living in a spacious apartment in a wealthy part of town, young Julio spent hours dawdling around the house with his mother and looking out onto the busy street life from the pristine privacy of his family's soaring wrought-iron balcony. A younger brother, Carlos, would join him on that very ledge eighteen months later.

Rich in history and overflowing with culture, Madrid is the kind of city one can get lost in. Strolling through its narrow streets, stopping for a *chato*, a glass of red or white wine before dinner, cheering at the bullfights—these are just some of the attractions that await the accidental tourist and greet the permanent resident.

For all their worldly advantages, the Iglesias family was not what one would call entirely functional. From an early age, young Julio was aware of difficulties in his parents' marriage. The rumors of his father's sexual exploits with other women would at first shock his delicate constitution, and then alter it beyond recognition. With time, he would learn to justify the infractions, growing closer and closer to his father as he grew up.

On the surface, the family operated like a well-oiled machine. Rosario would escort Julio and Carlos to school, and play the dutiful wife at home. On the inside, however, she was fuming with all the outrage of a woman scorned, and planning the rift that would ultimately divide the family forever.

The loyalties of the children would split down the middle (and here we anticipate the course of events). Given their present reputations—Julio Iglesias is alleged to have bedded more than 3,000 women since the time he was twenty years old, while his younger brother, Carlos, has remained with one woman for a number of years—it's clear which parent each brother sided with in the ongoing war of the Iglesiases. While Carlos stuck by his mother, caring for her well into her twilight years, Julio formed a strong attachment to his father. But the disruption of the family would not occur until much later. Meanwhile, life went on for the Iglesias family as normal.

Ironically enough, the boy who grew into the quintessential "Latin lover" wasn't considered good-looking by his peers. He would often have to play second fiddle to Carlos, who received most of the attention from family and friends. Knowing that he would never be as handsome as his younger brother wrought a deep-seated insecurity in Julio, one that still plagues him to this very day.

Gabi Fominaya, a family friend from the old days, recalled that "Julio had quite an inferiority complex about his looks compared to Carlos. Carlos was an exceptionally beautiful child with thick dark hair and beautiful long eyelashes. I think Julio got sick of people saying how lovely his brother was."

No doubt Julio was affected adversely by the comparisons made between him and his brother. Although had it not been for his being deficient in the beauty department, Julio would never have striven to develop his personality. Using charm and wit to win the affections that his then-gangly and awkward frame could not, Julio developed the kind of social ease that would later help him ascend to the heights of international stardom.

He would also excel in the game of soccer, a sport

that was more like an institution than a pastime in Europe. If a young boy showed promise in soccer, one could feel certain that academics, girls, and popularity would all fall into place. Being a skilled jock was not something the Spanish took lightly, and Julio had been pushed to develop his gift since he was just five years old.

By his fifteenth year, Julio had become such a proficient goalkeeper that he decided to attend tryouts for Real Madrid, Spain's premier pro soccer team. Hundreds of young hopefuls had come to compete for the limited team slots, but it was Julio who was handpicked from the crowd to serve as the junior reserve goalkeeper. "From the outset Julio made it always look kind of easy," said Fernando Valls, a fellow teammate. "He was a showman, you know. He would spin the ball around the tip of his finger before booting it back into play. He was agile and daring. He always went for the ball, even in the most impossible situations. He definitely had what it might have taken to go all the way to the top."

Although Julio couldn't have known it at the time, his desire to take center stage and show off for the crowd already suggested the magnificent future that awaited him in show business. Even then, he had all the makings of a superstar and a world-renowned performer. Since the very first time that he blocked a shot, he would forever crave the roar of an appreciative audience and the hush of a jam-packed stadium as he dove for the ball. Of course later, the soccer balls would be replaced by women's lingerie, and the audience of male sports fans by throngs of female admirers.

His old friend and current manager, Alfredo

Fraile, noted the immense impact that joining the team had on Julio's development. "After joining Real Madrid he became a kind of local hero—someone that people looked up to. Maybe that was his real taste of success and adulation and he never stopped needing it."

To anyone with neither the time nor the inclination to probe deeper, Julio was on top of his game and on top of the world. When he turned twenty years old, he was on his way to becoming one of the brightest stars on the Real Madrid roster, as well as earning his law degree at the Colegio Mayor de San Pablo.

As a young man, Julio was not apt to rock the boat. He was well aware of the respect his soccer skills elicited from his parents and friends. It was as if he were on a roll in the approval department, and was scared to slow down his momentum. To secure his position in his parents' good graces, Julio made plans to study law. Law would be his anchor, and soccer would be his crowning glory. "Like everybody, I wanted to be a doctor, lawyer, or engineer," he told *People* magazine.

His friends were known to say that Julio had life all figured out and neatly compartmentalized, but Julio was just beginning to find out what he was made of. In fact, although he claims to have chosen law as his profession, his father's not-so-subtle pressure tactics had exerted a tremendous influence on that decision. "I always wanted both my sons to be something in life," explained Julio Sr. "Carlos was an already exceptional student and it came easily to him. But for Julio, studying was always more hard.

He wasn't a natural like Carlos. But I insisted that at least he tried."

And try he did. Julio attempted to immerse himself in his studies, but would invariably find himself needing to take frequent breaks between his courses. After all, he was young, popular, good-looking, and a rising soccer star. What more need be said of youth and its zest for the fast life?

Living fast had always been Julio's motto. But this credo never proved as dangerous as it did on the night of September 22, 1963. Majadahonda was home to an annual fiesta that attracted young people from every corner of Spain; the equivalent of America's youth flocking to the shores of Panama City, Florida, for spring break. And much like any other young man released from the duties of school, Julio took advantage of the fiesta, dancing in the town's square, dining al fresco, and whistling at every pretty girl who passed him in the plaza.

Happy and carefree after a short-lived but satisfying romp, Julio and his two consorts jumped into his sporty Renault, ready to return to the real world. They had not been drinking, but even so, the giddiness they felt just from being young and alive intoxicated their senses. Julio was so high on life that he felt invincible, so invincible that he decided to test his courage by accelerating the car to 100 mph just as he was rounding a dangerous bend in the road. The car spun violently, as Julio tried desperately to regain control. But it was too late. The vehicle had teetered over a sharp precipice, plunging deep into the soil.

For a minute, Julio thought that he was done for. But no sooner had the car come to a crashing halt than he regained consciousness. He was still in the driver's seat and wasn't visibly injured. His passengers were also fortunate, escaping with only minor scrapes and bruises. Hobbling away from the site of the crash, the three shaken friends went in search of help. All was well, at least for the meanwhile.

In October of the same year, Julio returned to school with the intention of resuming his studies and his practice sessions as a member of Real Madrid. Anxious to get out on the field and prove his mettle to his coaches, Julio ignored the slight discomfort in his spine. Because the pain was intermittent and would vary in intensity, Julio eschewed the doctor's office, hoping that the problem would go away of its own accord.

Instead of improving, however, the discomfort grew stronger. Performing routine blocks and lunging for the ball became increasingly difficult. Soon the pain would prevent him from playing altogether. The strain on his spine had gotten so bad that he could barely stand up straight, let alone jump head-first to block a shot.

"Julio came to me and complained of this weird pain, which was obviously becoming worse by the day," recalled Julio Sr. "He was gray with pain. He was dying with it. For a father to see his son this way is a terrible thing. He had always been a healthy boy—an athlete. But I could see the gravity of his condition written on his face. I ran to every specialist that I knew and called in every favor I was owed to try to find out what was wrong with him."

Getting to the root of the problem would be easier said than done. Without the medical advancements of the past twenty years, diagnosing Julio's spinal discomfort proved to be a challenge of immense proportions.

One doctor after another would shake his head after examining the stricken young man. And even though they witnessed his pain firsthand, they could find nothing wrong with him. Some specialists even went so far as to suggest that the problem was all in his head. Julio Sr. would not stand to have his son so disparaged. He was so angry with the doctors' ineptitude that if he hadn't been one himself, he surely would have written off the entire profession as a racket.

Days turned into weeks and weeks into months, and still there was no answer. When the New Year had come and gone, and Julio's malady was no closer to being cured, Julio's father took matters into his own hands. He secured the aid of some of Spain's most renowned neurosurgeons, begging them to diagnose his son. Through a painful procedure called the Tiodoro, the team of doctors promised to catch what the myriad of X rays had missed.

Hopeful as Julio's father was about detecting the problem, the new procedure was extremely dangerous and painful. In his autobiography, Julio described the extreme anxiety he felt during the operation. "I think it was for me the greatest moment of anguish I have ever experienced. The moment of my greatest fear, my greatest sense of being a complete nobody, of feeling all the fear of a small child or of a small animal. I have been a hyper-strong kid, super strong . . . I had been one of the best sportsmen my school had ever had. I was a complete sportsman. I was an athlete from head to toes, but there I was with liquid moving slowly down my spine with my head bowed. Like a rabbit, like a bull, like a ewe about to be put to death in a slaughterhouse."

Grim as his thoughts were at the time, the reaper of souls would not make an appearance on that day. As if to make up for all the anguish he experienced while lying prostrate on the table, the procedure proved successful. It finally provided the Iglesiases with the answers they had been searching for. "You could see the problem clearly," Dr. Iglesias revealed. "A soft cyst had been growing on Julio's spine and causing gradual paralysis by compressing the verte-brae and the nerves."

No sooner had Julio's family breathed a long-overdue sigh of relief than they were confronted with an even bigger problem than uncertainty—Julio was paralyzed from the waist down. He would have to stay at the hospital for a new round of treatments.

Fifteen days would pass until Julio was allowed to go home. But this would not be the happy home-coming he had envisioned. The doctors were once again baffled by the young man's paralysis, leaving the family no other option than to buy a wheelchair for their son, something they had tried to postpone for as long as possible.

Seeing the wheelchair for the first time was just about as traumatic for Julio as his father had antic-ipated. No matter how hard he tried to wrap his mind around it, Julio could not understand how he, the soccer whiz, the strong athlete, could wind up in a wheelchair.

Julio would have plenty of time to accept the cruel hand life had dealt him. Bedridden and despondent, he would need every minute of those painful months to recuperate from the blow and regain his strength.

As a testament to his prowess, Julio started working on a strict regimen of mind over matter. He would spend hours communicating with his body, trying desperately to revive his listless form. "One day I was a guy full of strength," he expressed to *People* magazine. "And the next I was completely paralyzed. I learned how to control the pain in the muscles. I spent hours and hours a day giving orders to my brain: Move my fingers, my arms, my feet."

Four months of repeated effort would not prove fruitless. His will to walk again was so powerful that he began feeling sensation in his toes, then in his knees, and then in his entire leg. Although he would need to engage in a grueling round of physical therapy sessions, Julio was well on his way to a complete physical recovery. His emotional recovery, however, would take much longer than he'd ever expected.

By 1966, Julio had gained enough control of his body to move around with the aid of a walking stick. It would take another two years for him to walk on his own. Of course, a slight limp would always remain to remind him of the horrible ordeal—as if he could have ever forgotten.

"Though even now you notice with Julio that when he's onstage he can often look shaky and unstable," commented Alvaro Rodriguez, a photographer who shot Julio on several occasion. "People have even sometimes commented that he looks a little drunk—which is never the case; he is simply not secure on his feet. It's for this reason that he likes to wear special shoes on stage that have very thin, clothlike soles that allow him to grip the ground. If you look at his feet, he uses them like claws to hang on to the ground."

*   *   *

After regaining his motor functions, Julio wanted nothing so much as to make up for lost time. He had spent a large part of his youth rehabilitating at home, and was bent on experiencing all of the pleasures that life had to offer, including outings with friends and with women. Not surprisingly, his father's wish that he go back to school fell on deaf ears. "I've got a lot of living to do," was the crux of Julio's retort. And after seeing his son's struggle to walk, Julio Sr. didn't have the heart to protest.

For the next couple of years, England would be the place Julio called home. Given the young man's desire to brush up on his English and fend for himself, the UK was the perfect choice. Ever since the accident, confidence had become an issue of paramount importance to the young man. He'd lived under the supervision and protection of his family for so long that he began to question his resolve to make a mark on the world. England was far enough away that he would not be tempted to call home for moral and financial support. Whether he could stomach the separation was another matter altogether.

As a student at the Bell Language School in Cambridge, Julio was a stranger in a strange land. With no money and no friends, the young man realized that he had taken on more than he was capable of handling. He felt utterly desolate and alone until he met fellow Spaniard Enrique Bassat. Julio jumped at the chance to open up to Enrique, telling him of his unfortunate situation in England.

"Okay, you can come with me," said Enrique, unable to repress his urge to help out. "You can share my room and you can share my money," he continued, "and we'll both live on what I have until the situation improves."

Inseparable from that point on, Enrique and Julio would remain friends for many years to come. Eventually, the latter would even name his son after the friend whom he credited with turning his life around. In Julio's darkest hour, Enrique had arrived like a saving grace. Just knowing that he would have a roof over his head and a companion to talk with put Julio in a better frame of mind. Of course, money would be tight for the down-on-their-luck duo. If they wanted to eat, let alone keep their tiny studio apartment, they would have to come up with a money-making scheme, pronto.

Since his days as a soccer star, Julio had not shown a proclivity for other activities. He enjoyed singing, but after being laughed off the field by his soccer buddies, Julio kept his vocals relegated to the safe confines of the shower. When pressed by his ever-industrious friend, however, Julio admitted to having sung a clear note in his day, as well as to having a rudimentary knowledge of the guitar. And as beggars couldn't very well be choosers, Enrique responded to Julio's admission by booking him a gig at the Airport Pub. At first, Enrique and Julio began playing as a duet. But once he became aware of Julio's talent and the incredible impact his performances had on the audience, Enrique graciously bowed out, giving his new friend center stage.

"I would go with him most weekends and I also started drumming up business in other pubs, too," explained Enrique. "We used to play at one in Ely just outside Cambridge. Julio would sing songs that were popular at the time—Tom Jones, Engelbert

Humperdinck, The Beatles—and people responded to him because he had something then that he still has now, something you can't really quantify. He had a kind of light that shone from him. A kind of charisma."

When Julio first heard the resounding applause of the audience, it was as if he was right back on the old soccer field. The hard-won confidence he had gained during his stint with Real Madrid, and then lost during his extended convalescence, came flowing back as if by magic. He became so self-assured that he even found the courage to do what he'd once thought impossible—to fall in love.

Gwendoline Bollore was the kind of girl Julio could not resist. Unfortunately, with her blond hair, high cheekbones, and regal air, other men would also find her irresistible—namely Enrique, who had fallen in love with the young lady long before Julio ever came on the scene. When she showed an interest in Julio, young Enrique was crushed by the blow. More importantly, he felt slighted by Julio who had gone out with her on the sly to avoid the inevitable confrontation.

Painful as the discovery of the clandestine relationship was to bear, Enrique's loyalty toward Julio didn't waver. As a testament of his enduring fealty, he even went the extra mile by joining the new couple on their many excursions around town. His was a friendship that Julio would never forget. "I knew I was the loser, but I kept the feeling inside myself," Enrique would later lament. "Julio understood it and Gwendoline understood it. But we carried on, the three of us, the best of friends, because I couldn't bear to lose the friendship of either of them. But Julio understands that I had to sacrifice a very important thing in my life at the time for the sake of friendship—Gwendoline—and I know that he has never forgotten that."

Even then Enrique knew that Julio was a man of action, a man who would achieve anything he set his mind to, no matter what the circumstances. Even if he wanted to, going against Julio would be much like fighting a riptide—futile and utterly exhausting.

Although Enrique had forsaken his first love to Julio, he might have thought twice about it had he known that the young balladeer would relinquish the prize soon after the thrill of the conquest had waned. It wasn't long after he fell in love with the fair Gwendoline that Julio sparked to another challenge. He vowed to become a famous singer.

Encouraged by Gwendoline's love and affection, Julio scrounged up what remained of his little savings and recorded *"La Vida Sigue Igual"* (Life Continues Just the Same), a song he had written on his own and sung on countless occasions. Thinking he had no chance of breaking into the business, he sent the demo off to a couple of record labels. To his surprise and utter elation, Columbia came calling. Not only did they want him to record the song, they also promised to enter him into Benidorm, a competitive showcase for up-and-coming artists.

In July 1968, Julio took first place in the prestigious competition. It would be his first step in a long line of musical victories, and the last of his moments with his first true friend and his first true love. "We'd heard him sing '*La Vida Sigue Igual*' a million times and we thought it was a pretty song," said Enrique.

"But we didn't stop to consider how it might change his, and our lives."

Julio obviously hadn't either. But it was just as well, for nothing could have prepared him for what would follow.

The years that Julio Iglesias would spend in racking up countless record sales and sexual conquests are important to Enrique's story only in that they would reveal the loneliness and solitude that would characterize his formative years. In the ten years after he said good-bye to his shy, insecure self, Julio would go on to perform 200 shows per year for $250,000 each and sell more than 100 million albums worldwide. His musical career would span generations, cultures, and language barriers. And for that he had a right to be proud. "It's a nice way to live, no?" he boasted to a reporter. "It is a nice way to live, yes. How can I not love what's happened to me, how lucky I am? I love to be Julio Iglesias."

Although his career was an obvious source of gratification, there were other aspects to his life, many of which Julio could not take pride in. His marriage to Isabel Preysler, a Filipino beauty, was one of them. From the first moment he laid eyes on the exotic young woman in May of 1970, Julio was determined to have her for himself. She had the rare elegance, naivete, and porcelain good looks that Julio prized in women. His first reaction was to reach out and protect her from the harsher realities of life, the same cruel truths that, ironically, his later behavior would inevitably succeed in imposing upon her. But who could deny the pull of beauty, youth, and ambition? Certainly not Isabel. After a brief whirlwind of a romance, the couple was married on January 21, 1971.

The ceremony was one of the most elaborate and widely publicized in all of Spain. By then, Julio had amassed a significant following and was considered to be one of the country's premier entertainers. It was a romantic wedding, offering promise and hope for the newlyweds, and anyone else who was lucky enough to be invited to this most exclusive party of the year. With rosy visions of eternal joy and matrimonial bliss dancing in his head, Julio was overheard saying before the ceremony, "I'm happy to be about to marry the woman of my dreams. I don't think it's her beauty I fell in love with. It was her goodness that struck me. And as for Isabel, I don't think she fell in love with a famous singer, but with a simple normal guy, Julio Iglesias."

True enough, Isabel had not married Julio for his showbiz success, but in spite of it. As for the part about Julio being a simple, normal man with humble needs, nothing could have been further from the truth.

Ever since the accident that almost left him paralyzed, Julio had a voracious appetite for everything life had to offer—money, good wine, expensive cars, and beautiful women. Although he vowed to be faithful to his young wife, Julio would not make good on that promise.

No sooner had Isabel given birth to their first daughter, Isabel (nicknamed Chabeli) on September 3, 1971, than Julio began the pattern of absence that would ultimately contribute to the demise of their marriage. Dividing his time between tours and recording studios, Julio arrived at the hospital several days after his first child had been brought into the world. Try as she might to make the best of his tardiness, Isabel had already unwittingly accepted her fate.

"Well, he was working, he was on tour, which was the way it always was, and because of that he could only stay for a couple of hours," she would later explain the circumstances surrounding her first delivery. "But yes, yes, that hurt a lot even though in a funny way it also gave me strength because I thought, 'Well, I have given birth alone, so I can be a mother, father . . . I can be everything.' "

Whether Julio was already in the throes of his many amorous side-projects wasn't certain, it would take many years until Isabel became aware of the infidelity that was by then a widely known fact. Yet, how could Isabel have known when Julio protected her not only from the prying eyes and wagging tongues of the media, but from her closest confidants as well? He had become so possessive and domineering that he would even go so far as to forbid her from going out with her girlfriends. "Everything was a big deal . . . I needed to take my driving test in Spain and because the instructor was a man, that was a big deal," Isabel explained. "If I wanted to go and play tennis it was a big deal, too. If I wanted to go out for the night with a girlfriend in Madrid that was unthinkable."

As a result of having devoted so much of her time and energy to pacifying Julio's green-eyed monster, she had completely lost sight of the fact that maybe she too had something to be jealous about. Isabel reflected, "Well, how could I imagine that someone who was so concerned with my fidelity could be unfaithful to me? And his concern was so intense that I genuinely felt that he needed to get some help with it."

The trusting wife's suspicions of Julio's marital crimes and misdemeanors were further offset by her preoccupation with the care and upbringing of her daughter and newborn son, Julio Jose, who was welcomed into the world on April 23, 1973.

On May 8, 1975, just a little more than two years after her second pregnancy, the hero of our story, Enrique Iglesias, would make his first appearance. By now, Isabel was known to half jokingly remark that she would be barefoot and pregnant for the entire duration of her marriage to Julio. Alas, Enrique would be her last gift to the man who had everything.

Unbeknownst to the bearer, however, this gift would never truly belong to its intended recipient. Even as his mother held the crying infant in her arms, she couldn't shake the feeling that instead of heralding a new beginning, Enrique's birth would ultimately be the harbinger of the end for her and Julio. Although Isabel didn't know as much herself, she had fulfilled her wifely obligations, and would soon be moving on to the next phase of her life. Still, she couldn't shake the feeling that little Enrique was somehow penetrating the innermost recesses of her mind, and seeing the future that she herself was too scared to acknowledge. It was this deeply hidden truth that her infant son was born to carry in silence.

Much like the aptly titled album, *A Mexico* (For Mexico), which was completed only days before his youngest son's birth, Enrique was born for the world, for a greater purpose that he would not truly understand until much later in life. He belonged to no one and to everyone. An orphan who would only feel at home within the music that gave him both life, and a reason to live it.

T W O

Silent All These Years

By all appearances, Julio Iglesias was a happily married family man. Posing with his lovely wife and three beautiful children, he was the very image of domestic tranquility and parental affection. But the façade was as ephemeral as it was deceptive. On those rare occasions when he could be found at home with his family, Julio would play the doting husband and father with all the conviction that his failed acting attempts had lacked. However, during the majority of the time that he spent on the road, Julio was a completely different man.

In all fairness, Julio's infidelity to Isabel was neither a source of shame nor pride. It was just a fact of life that he'd picked up from his own father, who had freely admitted to having had girlfriends on the side. "Boys will be boys" was Julio's rationale for his behavior, and the fact that he was free to be as "boyish" as he wanted to be didn't hurt any either.

In 1977, Julio was at the peak of his musical and

sexual prowess. Not surprisingly, the two always seemed to go hand in hand. The more passion he infused into his lyrics and the more records he sold, the more women chased him through airport terminals and crowded streets. Lonely and exhausted after a grueling day of rehearsals and performances, Julio would often retire to his solitary hotel chamber only to discover beautiful, half-dressed women hiding in his closets and bathrooms. Now what man could honestly resist such temptation? All-too-human and not a little self-conscious from his old days, Julio often lost himself in the loving arms of the fairer sex.

Not once did his family ever figure into any of it. Despite his absences and infidelity, he loved his wife and children deeply. The challenge was to never allow the two worlds to collide. Julio avoided talking about his family with any of his girlfriends. According to him and the women who claimed to have dated him, the subject was strictly off limits. One former lady friend recalled the obvious omission, "But there wasn't a photograph of them anywhere—not even by the bed. And he never talked about them, which I thought was strange."

Julio succeeded in concealing all traces of his family life from his visitors. Unfortunately, he managed this task all too well. Without the constant reminders of his wife and children, he would lose sight of his familial obligations. Out of sight, out of mind was the unforeseen outcome of his dual existence. And since most of his time was spent touring, he spent far more time living the life of Julio the Latin lover and entertainer than Julio the loving family man.

"In most cases the blame for a divorce is fifty–fifty by the two people involved," reflected Alfredo Fraile,

Julio's manager and close confidant. "But in this case I think the majority of it was the fault of Julio. Julio and I were the same in this. Maybe, later, I took more care of my wife and family. But in those days we didn't care too much. We thought that if we sent them money, they didn't need anything more, and Julio knows now that this was not enough, he knows that it was his fault. Isabel was a very good wife and a very good mother and he knew when they separated that he had made a mistake."

Tabloid journalist had been breaking stories of Julio's trysts for as long as Isabel remembered being married to him, but like all famous people accustomed to living in the public eye, she never paid these rumormongers much attention. If Julio was indeed cheating on her, she figured that he would just come right out and tell her. For years, she went on believing this. Finally, after a friend tipped her off to a recent indiscretion, Isabel decided to get the matter straightened out once and for all. "I told him I knew about it and also I added that I knew about all the others, too—though, in fact, at the time I didn't," she said. "I suppose I wanted to see how he would react. And he didn't deny any of it, which was rather devastating. He simply said, 'But you know you were the only one that mattered, you were the only one that I ever really loved.' "

Julio might very well have thought that Isabel had known the truth all along. Although they never talked about them openly, he assumed that word of his infidelities had reached her ears. Isabel, on the other hand, was a trusting and kind woman, who wouldn't have dreamt of suspecting the worst of her husband.

He had been everything to her, and now the marriage was over.

Isabel was in a hurry to tie up the loose ends of her life, but Julio would not give up so easily. He was simply not ready to accept the dissolution of his marriage. To accept his fate would be to accept defeat. And that was something Julio could never do. Well, not yet at least.

To mollify her vexed husband and pay homage to everything they had shared during their eight-year marriage, Isabel agreed to a trial separation. She figured life wouldn't change that much, seeing that the couple had gotten used to being apart for long periods of time. The only difference was that now Isabel could go off and do as she pleased. She would not have to endure any more of Julio's late-night consultations and loving suggestions. Isabel was at last her own woman. "I told him that, as far as I was concerned, from that moment I was going to live my life and he would have to accept that. We didn't separate right away—basically because Julio refused to separate. So we had an arrangement whereby he was going to live his life and I was going to live mine. He never told me what he was going to do and I didn't tell him."

Gradually, the temporary peace pact began to hinder Isabel's mobility. Her every move had become fodder for the tabloids. The press's insinuations that she was cheating on Julio were unfounded. The young woman was simply stepping out on the town for the first time without Julio by her side. Alas, the red flags had been raised, and Isabel had no choice but to demand an annulment of her marriage in order to curtail the media's open-season approach to her formerly private personal life.

In 1978, divorce was still illegal in Spain. Isabel, however, was not without options. Wealthy Spaniards in need of a quickie divorce could procure their freedom by becoming US residents and paying a hefty sum. And that's exactly what Isabel and Julio did. Once all the papers had been signed and sealed, the couple went public with their statement in *Hola!* magazine. It read as follows:

> "To avoid possible speculation or scandalous news items that could arise from our personal situation, we both feel obliged to explain once and for all our decision, which has been arrived at by mutual consent and of our own free will, to legally separate. Above all, our chief concern, which is for our children, obliges us to resolve our personal situation in an amicable and legal fashion. The reasons for our separation, being personal and intimate ones, will always remain private."

As with any divorce, however amicable, the children were of paramount concern to their mother. Already three years old, Enrique was bound to feel the impact of the separation. His father might have been missing in action, but it was the distress of his mother that signaled that something had gone terribly awry.

Of course, even during those early years, Julio would not play a major role in Enrique's life. He was the ubiquitous phantom, whose presence was always felt, if not seen. Immature and young as he was, Enrique still felt abandoned by his father, but it was not his style to complain or to make unreasonable demands to see him. Isabel's love and affection was all he needed, or so he thought. It would take years for the young man to realize that the absence of a father figure had created a permanent void he could never fill.

In an attempt to justify Julio's prolonged absences, Isabel explained, "He did love his children. I can assure you of that. But he loved them in his own way. He loved them but you know, let's face it, Julio doesn't really like children. I can't say he was a bad father, but he never cared personally for them. That was my job. If they were sick, if they weren't sick . . . He never played with them either or took them out on Sundays. He wasn't that kind of father."

Julio admitted as much himself during an interview with Jane Oddy, saying, "My profession is the most important thing in my life. If I said that my family and my children were more important, then I would be lying."

Watching the neighborhood kids greeting their fathers after a long day's work, being lifted in the air in an affectionate embrace, or stepping out for fun-filled outings at the beach or park couldn't have been easy on Enrique. While the other kids walked off hand in hand with their fathers, he would hold his head high, gripping tightly to his mother's flowing skirts as he stumbled proudly along the street. When Julio did arrive for a brief stay, he would look at Enrique, beam with pride, and then send him off to play with his siblings. At the time, the three-year-old had no idea what his dad did for a living, but to his young, unformed mind it seemed that it had to be something special and grand. Why else would his father leave him behind?

Julio and Isabel's divorce would not make a lasting impression on the young boy. Isabel retained ownership of the family apartment in Madrid and a villa on the Costa del Sol. What's more, the terms of the annulment provided her with 200,000 pesetas a month for each child. All of Enrique's needs would still be provided for, except the one that had never been and would never be completely fulfilled—his need for a father.

His siblings, however, would provide a welcome distraction for the young boy. Chabeli and Julio treated Enrique as any older siblings would. They taunted him, teased him, and, most importantly, protected him. Enrique was known to pitter-patter after his older brother and sister, always trying to involve himself in their play. From riding their bicycles through the busy streets to playing in the local parks, the three children were never far from one another. But underneath the silvery peals of laughter and cheerful smiles lay a reality that was far more grim and depressing than anyone could have suspected. Theirs was a companionship built by necessity and the pangs of perpetual loneliness. And it was through their individual sorrows and disappointments that they understood each other implicitly.

Enrique was confronted by another transition in the beginning of 1979, when his father announced that he would be taking up permanent residence in America. On the lookout for a chance to penetrate the American marketplace since 1976, Julio took his divorce from Isabel as a sign to start anew. To the world, he presented a brave and stoic front. Inside, he was still reeling with doubts and insecurities. The rupture of his marriage had left him desolate and utterly alone. Spain only served as a reminder of his former failures, while America represented the promise of a new life.

To further mark the new beginning, Julio also embarked on a liaison with a young blond beauty of aristocratic descent, Virginia Sipl. Ironically, he chose her for her resemblance to his first love, Gwendoline. It was as if Julio was determined to prove something by correcting the mistakes of the past. He was a man on a mission, and nothing was going to get in his way.

A challenge was just the thing to get Julio's mind off his family. And making an English language crossover was just about as difficult a task as he could attempt. "When I came to America I was successful all over the world," he asserted. "But they don't care about that here. If it's not happening here, forget it. You can be number one in China, but forget it."

Julio would persevere once more. To commemorate his new presence on the American music scene, the singer erected what could be construed as a shrine to his own greatness. Set in a lush, tropical garden in an exclusive area of Miami, the house was a monument to all of the riches and splendor that the city had to offer. Blue swimming pools, tennis courts, and expansive lawns on which to play golf or cricket were staples of all the neighborhood's glorious abodes. Julio would not settle for second best. He wanted the house to express everything he was and could be, a completely self-contained pillar of strength. But as with his own personal development, a great many resources would have to be committed to the project. Luckily, money, unlike the insight and commitment needed to cure his emotional turmoil, was always in abundance.

Julio was bent on building an estate that would confound the visitor with its utter magnitude. At one point, Julio even ponied up $15,000 for a single tree. Virginia, who had moved in with Julio and was helping him decorate the house, had been overseeing the project. If she hadn't paid the contractors herself, she would have had a hard time believing how much money Julio spent on everything from the indoor and outdoor pools to the coconut trees framing the manor.

Indian Creek was the perfect setting for a family. And it seemed that Julio had every intention of spending time with his children. He put careful thought into the design and construction of their rooms, even going so far as to install an indoor swimming pool steps from their bedrooms. Enrique and the rest of his children had never been far from his mind. Indian Creek was a compound that needed a family to give it life. To that end, their parents arranged to have the three kids spend the summer with Julio, and the rest of the year with their mother.

Custody issues had never come between Isabel and her ex-husband. Isabel always promised to do what was in the best interest of her children, and she was not about to break her vow. She knew how important it was for Enrique, Julio, and Chabeli to see their father, and she never begrudged Julio his rights as a father. "There is none of that, 'They're mine' or 'Now it's my turn,' " said Isabel. "For my part I understand perfectly that it means a lot to Julio to have his children with him, just as I recognize that they also need to be with him."

Isabel also had her hands full with her new husband, Marques de Grinon, and daughter Tamara. While her decision to remarry had been one of careful deliberation, the children were upset by the transition. Having harbored hopes of a reconciliation between their mother and father, they were reticent to give up on their childish fantasies. Chabeli was most affected by her mother's marriage. Julio recalled in a 1988 interview, "The first reaction of any child is just to put the two parents together again. She did everything she could to put mother and father together. She cried and cried and cried. Now she is very understanding. But to understand is not enough. She does not try to make me feel guilty. None of us understand why it happened."

At first, Enrique was also adversely affected by his mother's second marriage. But unlike his older siblings, he had never indulged in any delusions about his father. He loved him dearly, but had never had the time to form a serious attachment.

In the end, the Iglesias children put their mother's happiness before their own. After all, how much different could their new stepdad be from their father?

Visiting the Indian Creek compound was always something Enrique and his siblings would look forward to with great anticipation. Although their stay would not put them in closer proximity with their father, who was still touring relentlessly, they were given ample opportunity to do as they pleased. Roaming the carefully tended grounds and playing tennis on the courts, Enrique was never so happy as he was during those carefree times. Despite his father's absence, the idea of coming to America took root in the young boy's febrile imagination.

Almost as if to compensate for Julio's truancy, Virginia Sipl gladly took up the slack for the overworked singer. Without children of her own, Virginia embraced Enrique, Julio, and Chabeli as if they were her own flesh and blood. Extremely lonely from having been left alone by Julio, Virginia needed the emotional outlet that his children provided. She would take any opportunity to entertain them, with frequent trips to amusement parks and boat rides. She was young, vital, and full of ideas, and the Iglesias kids responded to her as they would have to anyone who would put so much effort into their care and supervision.

Instead of resenting Virginia for taking his mother's place alongside Julio, Enrique treated her with almost the same warmth and affection as he did Isabel. Whether this behavior was a testament to the young boy's loneliness and need for attention, or a tribute to the vitality and humor of the new woman in his father's life wasn't clear. What was certain, however, was that Enrique was never as content as when he was in her company.

The years between 1978 and 1981 would progress in relatively normal fashion. Enrique was splitting his time between Madrid and Miami, and coming into his own as a young man. He had entered school, and was, for the first time, interacting with other kids his age. Surprisingly well-adjusted and self-assured for one who'd suffered so many childhood woes, Enrique's humor, candor, and liveliness were a constant source of pride for his mother. No matter how busy Isabel was in her old role as a socialite and her new role as a journalist, her face would always light up at the sight of her youngest son.

All seemed to be going smoothly on the Spanish front, but on December 20, 1981, something so devastating, so unfathomable would happen, that it would shake the Iglesiases' lifestyle to its very foundations.

After a routine afternoon spent catching up on his paperwork, Julio's father—Enrique's grandfather, who was now sixty-six years old—had begun the short walk back home. At three o'clock in the afternoon, Dr. Iglesias heard two men calling his name. When he turned around and asked them to state their business, he discovered that they were cameramen working on a documentary of Julio for a West German production company. Unable to resist helping his favorite son, Dr. Iglesias cordially agreed to accompany the men to a nearby café. There, he would be able to sit down and set the record straight about his talented boy.

But Dr. Iglesias would not get the chance to speak on his son's or his own behalf. Because only moments after he agreed to the interview, a car came screeching out of nowhere. Before he even had a chance to turn around, the two men had him bound and gagged, and were pushing him toward the car. Unable to break through their restraints, Dr. Iglesias was dragged, struggling, into the car.

Drugged and beaten by the assailants, Enrique's grandfather was taken to a hideout in a small town outside Madrid. He was then transported to another place he could not identify. Dr. Iglesias was scared stiff. He knew neither the identity nor the intentions of his assailants. Too exhausted by the drugs to struggle or beg for his freedom, he had no recourse except to lie down and conjure up the worst-case scenarios. Death, torture, mutilation—anything was possible. And the longer he was isolated, the more frightened he became. Dr. Iglesias was so traumatized by the kidnapping, that there were times when he wished that his captors would take his life.

"Nobody spoke a word to me," Dr. Iglesias would later recall. "They would put food in front of me and that was all, but they never communicated or answered my questions. Perhaps they believed that if we began a conversation, I would talk them round and they would have to release me. I went half-crazy. There is nobody who had been liberated from a kidnap who doesn't come out of it half-mad. All the things that happened to me during the Civil War were chicken shit in comparison—I really can't think of a worse torture for any human being. To be kept in isolation. To have no one to communicate with at all. To believe at any moment that you are about to be killed. It is an unbearable experience."

When Isabel broke the terrifying news, Julio was seized by panic and fear. Like his father, who paced up and down his small room, he could not sit still. For the first time since his divorce from Isabel, he felt alone and out of control. What good was all his success when it put his nearest and dearest in danger? was the question running through his mind.

As the eleventh highest-paid entertainer on the *Forbes* list and one of the most high-profile celebrities of his day, Julio and his family were prime targets. Making a lot of money had been something

Julio prized. But now it was threatening his way of life. Two days after Dr. Iglesias was reported missing, the kidnappers, who turned out to be none other than the notorious Basque separatist movement, ETA, called and notified Julio and his brother Carlos of the required ransom. Julio readied the sums to be transferred and sat waiting to be notified by the perpetrators. The agonizing moments when he didn't know whether his father was dead or alive still remain and will haunt Julio for the rest of his life. "The two of them are more like close pals than father and son," Carlos described Julio and his father's relationship to the *Daily Mirror* during this time. "Julio cannot eat or sleep since it happened. He just paces up and down and jumps each time the phone rings. He's ready to do anything to get his father released safe and sound."

The release of Dr. Iglesias would come about in a way no one could have anticipated. While Julio was waiting for the call from ETA, antiterrorist troops had swooped down on the two-story shack where Julio's father was being held captive. The troops apparently had no idea that Dr. Iglesias was being held there against his will, and were completely taken aback upon discovering the victimized man huddled in a corner.

News of Dr. Iglesias's release came from the Spanish Prime Minister. The entire country had been praying for the safe homecoming of Dr. Iglesias. Reunited in a tearful and much-publicized reunion at the airport, Julio clung to his father as if for dear life. Losing his father would have destroyed him, especially because he believed that he was ultimately responsible for the entire ordeal.

"Julio blamed himself for what happened to his father," Vivienne Ventura, a close family friend explained. "In the past he was so unconscious of security, but now he'll make pretty sure his family will never suffer like that again."

Indeed, Julio's efforts to protect his kindred bordered on the obsessive. A top-of-the-line security system was installed immediately and round-the-clock bodyguards were always on hand to protect his children during their summer visits. In 1989, Julio's paranoia had gotten so out of control that he even had Chabeli's boyfriends pass through security clearance before she could date them. But the last thing he cared about was looking foolish to the rest of the world. His family was going to be safe, end of story.

Back in Madrid, Isabel had also suffered deeply. After all, the kidnapping happened practically in her backyard. She had always kept tabs on her children's whereabouts, but that would no longer be good enough. Enrique was too young to recall his own emotions during that difficult time. But he was the most affected, in that, in a matter of a couple of weeks, his range of movement was significantly curtailed. Before, he was able to come and go as he pleased. Everyone from the butcher to the café owners knew who he was. Although Isabel had always felt secure in the knowledge that people were looking out for her young son, his visibility had suddenly become a liability.

In 1984, a nine-year-old Enrique, along with his siblings, was sent off to live with his father in Miami. The reasons for the move have never been determined. The kidnapping of Dr. Iglesias could have been the deciding factor. Isabel had expressed concern about her children's safety ever since Dr. Iglesias had come home. On the other hand, if she was so worried about their well-being, why would she have waited so long to send them packing? It could have been that Isabel simply wanted her children to learn English. Whatever the circumstances surrounding the move may have been, it was clear that Enrique, Julio, and Chabeli would now have a new place to call home.

To insinuate that the children were forced to move against their will would be ridiculous. Ever the devoted mother, Isabel would never have done anything without consulting her children first. To make the transition easier, their parents decided to make a trial relocation. Julio and Chabeli were already grown, and were fully capable of making their own decisions. "If we see they're not adjusting well, they'll come back earlier. If we see that they love it, then they could stay longer," Isabel reiterated her resolve in a later interview. "Everything will be done with the best interests of our children at heart."

Enrique couldn't have been too distressed upon hearing his parents' decision. He associated Miami with warmth, comfort, and serenity. Although he didn't know it at the time, his associations were centered less on the city itself than on the woman who made his visits so wonderful. Looking forward to seeing his old friend Virginia Sipl, Enrique didn't mind moving so long as she was there to keep him company. But a cold reality set in as soon as he arrived in Miami. His father informed him that Virginia had moved out. Shattered by the rumors of Julio's numerous affairs with the who's who of Hollywood, Virginia broke up with him once and for all, moving out of Indian Creek right before the children were scheduled to arrive.

Instead of one of those happy homecomings that Virginia had often orchestrated, Enrique arrived to an empty house, with only the staff to keep him company. This was not at all what he had expected. Distraught and disappointed, Enrique hid his feelings so he wouldn't upset his mother, who had called to check up on their safe arrival. His voice betrayed none of the pain of abandonment he was feeling. How was Isabel to know that when Enrique told her he was happy, he was anything but? Laughing on the phone and promising to be a good boy, Enrique hung up only to be swallowed up by the notion that, besides his brother and sister, he was entirely alone.

"It broke my heart to send them away," Isabel would later defend herself to *People* magazine, "but we had to for security reasons. If I had known that their father wasn't around, it might have been different."

THREE

Vital Signs

The loss of his mother's comforting presence would always weigh heavily on Enrique. Isabel
made a point of traveling to Miami at least twice a
year, but even then the young boy couldn't help sour-
ing the visits with thoughts of his mother's upcoming
departure. Still, for all of his frustration and loneliness, Enrique would never think of burdening her
with an admission of his state of mind. He loved
Isabel selflessly, and would never dream of upsetting
her with his mounting problems.

Because he had few people in whom he could con-
fide, his sense of isolation was only growing more
acute with the passage of time. He might have reconciled himself to the demands of his father's voca-
tion, but he had not anticipated that his sister would
also grow increasingly unreachable. Already thirteen
years old, Chabeli's career as a model in Spain was
just beginning to take off. Enrique envied her the
ability to visit their mother in Spain and to fly off to

see Julio whenever her heart desired. Too small and inexperienced to travel on his own, Enrique was anxious to grow up so that he, too, could spend time with his parents.

Finding himself in foreign surroundings, the young boy needed his mother's emotional support now more than ever. Since his previous visits to Indian Creek had resembled a summer camp experience, he had not prepared himself for a day when his father's home would be his own. To be quite frank, the only thing that had made his summer visits to Miami tolerable was seeing Virginia Sipl and the knowledge that he would be returning home to his mother. That notion had comforted and consoled him through many a sleepless night. And now that these hopes were gone, Enrique didn't quite know what to do with himself.

Adding to his general disorientation was the knowledge that he would have to start from scratch. All of his childhood friends were living in Spain, his English wasn't very good, and he had trouble assimilating in school. Had Enrique had a friend to whom he could turn, adapting to his new environment might have been easier. But as things stood, the young boy was forced to fend for himself, acquiring a maturity and composure that went way beyond his years. "Leaving my mother, it was very hard," Enrique explained to Diane Sawyer. "And having to start a new life, new friends, new school, different language. It wasn't easy. It was very hard."

The parental advice that most kids take for granted was what Enrique missed the most. Simply put, Julio was never around to guide the young boy's personal development. Subjects like the importance of good grades, sharing, and not bickering with his peers were never broached. His father was actually the last person Enrique would have come to for answers to his problems. But it wasn't so much that Enrique didn't love his dad, it was just that he didn't appreciate being made to feel like an unwanted burden. Proud from the day he was born, Enrique was very careful about giving more than he received. "If you have kids," he would later express in an interview, "you've chosen a responsibility. Be there for them. Don't leave them."

Of course, by dint of watching his father work in the studio or schmooze with the press, Enrique learned more than he could have ever realized. After all, his father had accomplished more than any other Latin artist who came before him. He had enchanted millions of people with his passionate lyrics. Surely, Julio contributed something to his son's education. Unfortunately, the virtues of hard work and dedication that Julio so expertly modeled for his youngest son are also responsible for the painful childhood memories that tug at Enrique's heartstrings to this very day. "I just saw him work hard," Enrique told the *Tucson Citizen.* "Hard work helped him advance from a little house to a bigger house to an even bigger house; from a bus to a plane to his own plane."

For all the benefits that came with this robust work ethic, Enrique would have gladly traded the fruits of Julio's labor for the chance to see his father more often. You see, no matter how much Enrique blamed his parents for being absent during his formative years, they were all he had. And the young boy tried desperately to maintain the already tenuous connection with frequent phone calls and plaintive letters. "I did miss them, but you get used to seeing your dad maybe once a month," he informed *People* magazine. "There was always a lot of communication between us, which helped a lot."

During those times when Enrique was left to his own devices, he could often be found visiting the household of Alfredo Fraile, Julio's manager. A good friend as well as a crafty business associate, Fraile was aware of the difficulties that were inherent in being born an Iglesias. Like everyone who met Julio, Fraile was not blind to the singer's good qualities, yet he was also painfully aware of his flaws. And as his children were visibly unhappy with their new environs, he made concerted efforts to show them that happiness and families could indeed go hand in hand.

Sure enough, Enrique's trips to the Fraile household were some of the most pleasant of his young life. He recalls playing with the children, and watching their mother cook dinner for the entire family. Enrique couldn't remember the last time his whole family had sat down for a hearty home-cooked meal. After dinner, Enrique would retire to the porch, where Alfredo would invariably be staging some form of entertainment for the kids. From playing the guitar to putting on elaborate dance numbers, Enrique was always up for the family's brand of merriment.

"I remember that Julio's children used to come to our house to be with us and our children and it was almost like they were our children, too," said Fraile. "They saw that the life at our house—a wife, a husband, and children—was stable and normal and they were attracted to that because it was not their experience and it was what they wanted so much. Everyone needs love and security—especially children. Julio tried hard to be with them in Miami and to spend time with them, but they needed more than that. They needed what all children need—a happy family life."

If Fraile had become Enrique's father figure, then Elvira Olivares, the children's nanny, had become their symbol of motherhood and nurturing affection. There were times when Enrique didn't know what he would do if it wasn't for the simplicity, warmth, and intelligence that he discovered in his caretaker. Chabeli and Julio were likewise smitten by Elvira, and the four of them would often spend their nights reading aloud and watching television. "I have never had children," Olivares revealed to *People* magazine. "But the love I have given these children has been a mother's."

There was a time when little Enrique may have craved the comfort that Isabel's presence provided, but as he matured, the young boy realized that life was what he made of it. If Elvira was offering her unconditional love, then he would embrace her with all the fervor of his little heart. Enrique was just waiting for someone to come along and love him, and when Elvira finally did, he treated her as if she was his own mother. The passage of time only served to strengthen the bond that would forever remain intact.

Dedicating his debut album to her is just one of the many proofs of affection that Enrique has shown Elvira. But in his opinion, it's the very least he could do for a woman who encouraged the discovery of his voice, his vision, and his undying zest for living life to the fullest. "She's given me so much, I should dedicate every album to her," he confided in *USA Weekend*. "Sometimes you've got to show that if it wasn't for a certain person, you wouldn't be where you are."

A loving and lively child, Enrique never failed to fill his nanny's heart with joy. He was everything she would have wanted in her own son had she found the opportunity to have one. But as things stood, Elvira's destiny was to raise the boy who would eventually mature into a world-famous singer. His nanny knew he was special, but she never could have suspected that Enrique would go on to accomplish all that he has. Even before he was able to sell out colossal stadiums in the span of just one day, Elvira was Enrique's staunchest and most loyal admirer.

Enrique's discovery of his nanny's selfless love for him came at the most opportune time. It seemed that his mother's visits were growing less frequent with each passing year. As a journalist, Isabel's job description required her to drop everything at any given moment, which she gladly did for the sake of her career. And although some onlookers were intrigued by her newfound ambition, those who knew her understood the underlying motives of her actions. After eight years spent in utter seclusion, tending to her children's every whim and need, the young woman was ready to actualize the dreams and ambitions she had put on hold for her family. And even though she never regretted a single moment of the time spent with her children or husband, she was determined to create an independent and strong identity that was all her own.

However, Isabel's involvement in journalism

could not drive a rift between her and Enrique, Julio Jr., and Chabeli. A day would not go by when she didn't think of her children, or check up on them. And even though he would have preferred to see his mother rather than talk on the phone, Enrique never forgot all the effort his mother exerted to make him feel loved and admired. If Elvira found a place in his everyday life, Isabel was also never far from his thoughts. They were the two most important women in his life, and for that Enrique would forever be grateful.

Still, loneliness continued to pose a problem for young Enrique. While it would seem to some that the young boy was born with a silver spoon in his mouth, Enrique never derived much satisfaction from his privileged lifestyle. No one could deny that the youngest Iglesias had all of the material advantages he would ever need. Lavish vacations, boats, and jets were just some of the things that he came to take for granted. Money was never something Enrique paid much attention to. After all, although he had more than he knew what to do with, it was precisely Julio's pursuit of wealth that lay at the root of his son's problems.

Most of the time, life at Indian Creek might have felt like a trip through an empty museum, but there were also those occasions when the manor was bustling with activity. Everyone from PR reps to show-girls to big celebrities would come to the house to visit with their favorite international sensation. And while watching his father hold court might have inspired great pride in the impressionable young boy,

Enrique never treated Julio with the veneration shown him by his fans and coworkers.

Julio was a god to anyone who was fortunate enough to penetrate his tight-knit circle. But in Enrique's eyes, his father was all too human. Of course, he understood that Julio was important. There was no doubt in his mind that his father could accomplish anything with the snap of his fingers. Yet for all his family's influence, Enrique would never fall prey to the trappings of celebrity. "It's just a part of my blood," he told CNN. "I don't look at it like he's a legend. It's just completely normal. I grew up with it. When you grow up with it, it becomes completely normal."

For all of Enrique's attempts to appear calm and nonchalant in the face of his father's immense success, there were times when even he, the incorrigible cynic, could not help feeling awed by Julio's strong sway over the music world. Michael Jackson's visit to Indian Creek was one of the few times that Enrique actually enjoyed being the son of Julio Iglesias. While most young people only dreamt about meeting the pop icon, Enrique had the chance to entertain him in his own house.

Taken completely unawares, the young boy stood still without saying a word. Staring up at the tall man in a red jacket, Enrique didn't need to see the famous rhinestone glove to know that this was indeed the very Michael Jackson who broke *Billboard* records with songs like "Billy Jean," "Beat It," and the ever-popular "Thriller." For the first time in his life, Enrique Iglesias was utterly starstruck.

Communication between Michael Jackson and Enrique was stunted at first, but gradually, Enrique got up the nerve to speak out. By the time Jackson had bidden the family adieu, the young boy had grilled him on everything from the making of the "Thriller" video to what he ate for breakfast. "When I was a kid, he came to my dad's house and stayed in the room next to mine," he recalled the incident to *USA Weekend*.

The perks of fame, however, weren't always that sweet. Ever since his father's kidnapping, Julio had realized that being a celebrity was not the answer to his woes so much as a catalyst for a whole new set of difficulties. "Being rich and famous does not get rid of your problems," he explained in 1988. "It just gives you new ones."

Security at Indian Creek was extremely tight. Enrique, along with his brother and sister, was not allowed to go anywhere unescorted. To Enrique, it seemed that it was hard enough growing up on his own, let alone having to do so in front of the entire world. Always watched and followed everywhere they went, the Iglesias children were forced to mastermind various escape plots in order to obtain some much-needed privacy.

As the eldest of the trio, Chabeli was the first to stage a breakout. Already in her teens, there was nothing she would have liked more than to hang out with her friends and boyfriends without the pestering of a meddlesome security guard. While her friends took mundane activities like shopping at the mall or hanging out at a restaurant for granted, Chabeli had to conceive elaborate schemes to secure her freedom.

Once she had learned to elude the security system of Indian Creek, there was the not-so-small matter of the paparazzi to contend with. Ruthless in their zeal for images of the oldest Iglesias beauty, photographers would camp out behind the gates, waiting to pounce on her as soon as she came into view. And although she laughs about these incidents today, her range of movement was considerably hampered by the press's insatiable curiosity.

"I would ride in the trunk of the car," she admitted to *People* magazine. "Once we were going along, and it was really bumpy, and I was hitting my head. And once I felt like I couldn't breathe anymore, and I started banging on the trunk, and the driver couldn't hear me. I thought I was going to die!"

Having had fame thrust upon her, Chabeli was impervious to its sundry charms. Celebrity was nothing but an inconvenience, a deterrent to doing the things that made her happiest. Of course, being the daughter of Julio Iglesias did have its advantages. Her attempt to launch a modeling career was just one of the instances when having the Iglesias name came in handy. But even though her professional life would always be full of opportunities, Chabeli, like her younger siblings, would have gladly traded it all in for some moments of peace and quiet. "Some people are just famous," she explained. "Like John F. Kennedy, Jr. He never did anything, and you ask yourself, 'Why do people like him?' Or Caroline of Monaco. The only thing she's done is get married twice. I don't know whether they're lucky or unlucky, but they get the limelight."

Much like Enrique, Chabeli also resented the limelight in that its only service was to keep her father remote and distant. She wouldn't have minded his profession so much except that it interfered with her family life. "He was always into his work," explained Chabeli. "When he had time, he was with us, but family was never his strong point."

FOUR

Of Joy and Sorrow

For better or worse, the Iglesias children had become skilled at fending for themselves. Chabeli had her modeling and friends, Julio Jr. had sports, and Enrique had at last found his true calling—music. "You know how some kids go play soccer, some kids go play football?" he asked. "I went to sing, and I loved it."

Like most adolescents who feel stifled, alone, and frustrated, Enrique needed a creative outlet for his pent-up emotions. The desire had sprung up back when he was in his seventh year. With no one to relate to except his nanny, brother, and sister, Enrique began writing down his thoughts in a journal made up of little scraps of paper. Whenever he had a painful recollection or was frightened by the thought of being alone, he would console himself with the outpouring of words. "It was something I always wanted to go into since I was a little boy," Enrique conveyed to the *Buffalo News*. "In fact, it was the only way I had to express myself. I had no-body to talk to; I'd pick up a piece of paper and write some lyrics."

While Enrique claimed that his father's career had nothing to do with his decision, it's hard to give cre-dence to the assertion. Despite feeling nothing but aggravation toward show business and all of its neg-ative repercussions on his family life, Enrique was hell-bent on becoming a singer.

Although he would never admit to as much, En-rique's ambition was clearly an attempt to get closer to his father. If he could sing, then maybe he would get as much attention as Julio, and, if he excelled, then Julio would have to stand up and take notice of him. Even though all evidence points to the con-trary, Enrique would rather eat his leather pants than admit to having been influenced by his father. "I'm not sure in a way because ever since I was small, I always wanted to be a singer," he told the *Chicago Sun-Times*. "I mean, even if my dad wasn't a singer, I just remember praying to be a singer."

Yet, to maintain that his ambition was activated solely by his father's career would be to do Enrique a grave injustice. One part of Enrique may have wanted to be like his father, but the other wanted nothing to do with his over-the-top musical persona and way of life. And therein lies the paradox: As much as making music had become a means of fol-lowing in his father's footsteps, it had also become Enrique's surest path to distinguishing himself and molding his own identity. The need to be like his father and, at the same time, be nothing like his fa-ther still conflicts Enrique to this very day.

Enrique could never shake the feeling that his life

was somehow special or unique. As the youngest heir to the Iglesias musical dynasty, the boy understood that his experience was fraught with intrigue, drama, and passion. Each life event, no matter how trivial, was recorded in his journal and lyrics, as if to say, "There will come a day when I will make something of myself, and share myself with the world."

Every day after school, Enrique would rush home with pen and paper in hand to record all of his innermost feelings and sensations. He couldn't wait to get home so he could climb in bed, flip the bedspread over his head, and scribble away to his heart's content. No matter what had happened to him at school or at home, he would always find a safe refuge in his music. "When I was fourteen, writing songs was like therapy," he told the *Milwaukee Journal Sentinel*. "You isolate yourself until twelve midnight and then you go to bed. If it's still good when you get up in the morning, you've really got something. All of my songs are completely autobiographical. I can say stuff in a song that I would never say face-to-face. Music has always been my thing."

Sharing his innermost thoughts and aspirations with others had become extremely difficult for Enrique. No matter how hard he tried, he could not find the strength to tell his parents about his aspiration to become a famous singer. The young boy had simply lost the ability to speak on his own behalf. Having reconciled himself to the fact that his wishes carried little weight in the Iglesias household, Enrique learned to repress the expression of his thoughts and desires. "I never really told anyone," he explained. "It was my own little secret, my own little getaway."

Music had also become his personal haven from everything that was unpleasant and complicated. Irrational as it was, Enrique feared that his parents would forbid him to sing if he ever told them. His love for music was just too great to ever take that chance. According to him, nothing and nobody could ever stand in his way. "When I was seven, I'd kneel in bed and pray I'd be a singer," he confided in *USA Today*. "But I'd never have made it if I'd told my parents. If I'd heard anything negative, I wouldn't have been able to stand it."

Saddened by this inability to share his deepest desires with his family but unwilling to waste his talents, Enrique sought out the assistance of strangers. Everything had to be done secretly. Unlike other teens, who would beg their parents for a guitar or music lessons, Enrique was determined to develop his musical gift on his own.

When he was fifteen, Enrique was old enough to realize that he needed help. Writing alone in his room might have been therapeutic, but it would never elevate him to the top of the charts. Even though asking his family for assistance was strictly off limits, he had no trouble seeking guidance elsewhere. In fact, Enrique had gotten so used to having all of his emotional needs fulfilled by the family's friends and staff that he actually felt more comfortable around people who were not related to him.

While walking home from school one day, Enrique heard music emanating from Little Havana, a popular local restaurant. His soul was immediately lifted, and he went in to find out the source of the beautiful melody. When Enrique strode in he found two men strumming guitars and singing. Grabbing a seat at one of the tables, Enrique let the music envelop him like a warm blanket. When he reflexively looked at his watch, he was shocked to find out that several hours had gone by.

Tired from the long set, the two men took a short break. They were sipping drinks at a nearby booth when they spotted Enrique looking longingly in their direction. It was as if he wanted to say something to them, but didn't have the nerve. Finally, Enrique approached the two gentleman, who turned out to be local musicians Mario Martinelli and Roberto Morales. At first, all he wanted was to thank them for making such beautiful music. But as he went on and on about their lyrical sound and expert guitar playing, Enrique became even more emboldened. He was not about to let this opportunity for advancement slip through his fingers.

Meandering for a few minutes from topic to topic, Enrique finally worked up the courage to ask the musicians to help him compose songs. At that point, Martinelli and Morales had no idea that the young man sitting in their midst was none other than Julio Iglesias's son. Still, they invited the eager teen to sing for them after school one day. If the boy had any talent, they figured, they would help him hone his sound. Conversely, they would have no qualms about giving him his walking papers if he was totally inept.

With a gleam in his eye and a clutch of scribbled-up papers in his hand, Enrique marched into Morales's tiny basement with the gait and proud bearing of a soldier going into a long-awaited battle. He knew he had his work cut out for him if he hoped to impress the two musicians. Singing a few bars as a warm-up, Enrique cleared his throat and launched into one of his medleys. It was his first time singing in front of an audience, and he would never forget it. "I started singing with poor musicians but they were very talented," he told *TV y Novelas*.

Morales and Martinelli did nothing to hide their pleasant surprise at hearing young Enrique sing. They patted him on the back, and commended him for a job well done. Of course, his delivery was by no means flawless; they would need time to work on that. But he did have a sonorous quality to his voice that was the mark of future success. They were shocked to find out that Enrique had had no prior vocal training, and were even more taken aback when the young boy finally revealed his famous last name. Although Enrique would avoid all conversations relating to his father's vocal prowess and commercial success, the two musicians could not help but see his father in everything he did.

Enrique had won his first supporters. He felt as if a major burden had been lifted from his narrow shoulders. No longer would he have to labor on his music alone. He may have gotten used to being his own number-one champion, but the recognition of professional musicians meant more to him than he could ever have imagined. From now on, Enrique would walk through his day with a lighter step and a lighter heart. Even his siblings noted the immense change that had come over the formerly sullen young man. Desperate to pinpoint the origin of his good cheer, they teased him about having a new girlfriend. But little did they know that Enrique had found something he had been looking for all along—inner strength and self-confidence.

Not a day went by without Enrique's racing to meet with Martinelli and Morales. The two men would become not only his private coaches, but his confidants as well. They did their best to instill their young protégé with confidence, but Enrique continued to suffer from recurring outbreaks of self-doubt. Inexperienced and still untrained, the adolescent would need to mature into a man before he could make the kind of music he could be proud of. "I used to cry about how bad they [the songs] sounded," he confided in the *Washington Post*. "That was the hardest point, getting used to my voice, getting used to feeling good about what I was singing and writing. It took a long time."

Eventually, Enrique's self-assurance began to blossom. But while his voice and manner of expression were no longer the sore points they once were, all of the confidence in the world could not make him reveal the nature of his after-school activities. He had sworn himself and his new tutors to absolute secrecy. By no means were they ever to tell anyone what he had been doing. Rumors had a way of spreading like wildfire around Miami, and if anyone had heard that Julio Iglesias's son was trying his hand at singing, it would have been in all of the local papers the next morning. And there was nothing that Enrique feared more.

Ever since the day Isabel first looked into her youngest son's eyes, Enrique had been a serious young boy. He had undergone painful separation anxiety, first from his father and then his mother, and was forced to deal with his grandfather's kidnapping at a young age. Suffice it to say, Enrique had had his share of troubles.

But morbid brooding was not Enrique's style. His happy face and bounding gait belied his somber nature then, just as his yen for life's pleasures obscured his weightier concerns when he entered his teens. He was young, attractive, and intelligent. There was absolutely no reason why he had to stay cooped up writing in his room all day. Luckily, he discovered a pastime that enervated his spirits and brought a smile to his fresh-scrubbed face. "When I was thirteen, I started windsurfing a lot in Miami," he told *Rolling Stone* in 1999. "That's the only sport I was really good at. I used to go to Hawaii for two months in the summer and live in a hut and just windsurf. Now, when I have a day off, I go waterskiing and scuba diving."

Surfing out of his emotional shell, however, would not prove to be as easy. Confined to a small and insulated world from a young age, Enrique had become shy and not a little withdrawn. As a high-school student at the Gulliver Preparatory School, a private learning institution located in a top-drawer section of Miami, Enrique was not exactly what one would call popular or socially adept. The two thousand students attending the prep school had all come from relatively privileged backgrounds, but Enrique's name was by far the most illustrious and well-known.

Unwilling to spend his life trying to live up to his father's standards, Enrique shunned the popularity that his brother's athleticism and sister's beauty had helped them enjoy. Because he had skills that he could not share with the world, his fellow students didn't know what to make of him. He wasn't a jock, a looker, or a performer. They had no idea what was going on in the mind of the sensitive loner, who was so unlike his siblings. But friendships were not as important to Enrique as the prospect of secluding himself in Morales's makeshift studio. He enjoyed some of his classes, especially history, but could never concentrate long enough to excel academically. Writing and singing songs were the only things that really mattered.

Enrique slept, ate, and dreamt music. Not a moment went by that he wasn't singing a melody to himself or mentally composing new lyrics. He spent hours locked up in his room, listening to his favorite artists. "I used to listen to a lot of Anglo acts—Fleetwood Mac, Dire Straits, Billy Joel, Journey, John Mellencamp."

The preference Enrique showed for the English language music scene had little to do with turning his back on his Latin heritage, and a lot to do with the fact that Latin radio stations were shutting out younger audiences. By playing only the older and more established Latin musicians, radio stations in Miami were preventing younger Latinos from taking over the airwaves. Like most of his peers, Enrique wanted to hear new sounds, and his early musical education was confined strictly to English albums. "You'd turn on the radio and think, 'What the hell is this?'" he explained to the *Washington Post.* "It's great to go back to our roots and to know where Spanish music came from and what it is, but it was people who were dead twenty years ago."

Despite the universal appeal of his father's music, Enrique could never get too jazzed over jamming along with the sounds of Julio Iglesias. In fact, it embarrassed him to hear his father singing plaintive ballads of love and lust. At that age, he had a hard time coping with his own burgeoning sexuality, let alone having to come to grips with the concept of his father's romantic life. The mere thought of his father's Latin lover status gave him a serious case of the heebie-jeebies.

The burden of having one of the world's most sexually active men for a father couldn't have been an easy one to bear. Whenever a mention of Julio's love life appeared in the press, Enrique would have to endure his fair share of teasing. Although he never confronted his dad about it, Enrique was affected by his parents' breakup and the sudden departure of Enrique's favorite childhood friend, Virginia Sipl. It was his firm belief that every woman he had ever loved had disappeared because of his father's inability to stay committed to one person.

Chabeli was also adversely affected by her father's relationship with women. She was so traumatized by Julio's attitude toward women that she even vowed to marry a man nothing like her father. "He's always been a womanizer," Chabeli revealed. "That's his life, and I've always said, 'I'm not getting involved in his life.' But I always looked for a husband who is not like my father."

Almost as if he was rebelling against Julio's Casanova reputation, Enrique made no efforts to please the ladies in school. Although many girls had secret crushes on the reserved young man, he never paid them much mind. Completely unaware of his discreet charms, the young boy went through high school believing that he was completely unattractive to the opposite sex. "I wasn't even close to popular, not even close," he told the *Milwaukee Journal Sentinel*. "I was on the low end. The moderate low end."

The thought of being labeled as just another chip off the old block frightened him. As a young boy, Enrique entertained romantic fantasies of meeting that one perfect girl that he could say anything to. And he worried that Julio's reputation would prevent him from finding the love of his life. Of course, that would never happen, because even before he became involved in a relationship, Enrique swore to himself that he would always be a one-woman kind of guy. "My father's a playboy," Enrique admitted to the *Tucson Citizen*. "If he's getting chicks, I'm happy. But it's not the kind of life I'd follow. If I have a girl, it's just that one."

FIVE

Here We Go!

High school was not something Enrique would ever wish to repeat. Instead of glory days, all-night parties, girls, and pep rallies, that time of his life was all about insecurity, painful self-analysis, and experimentation. As necessary as this period was for the formation of Enrique's artistic sensibility, he was anxious to establish himself as a well-rounded and sure-footed young man. With graduation in 1993 came a sense of closure. No longer would he have to rely on his parents for fulfilling his basic needs. He was finally independent, and that was all he ever wanted.

Still, the Iglesias name carried its own share of expectations and responsibilities. If Enrique hoped to make his family proud, then he would have to demonstrate his ambitions by attending college—or at least that's what his father thought. When Julio probed Enrique about his plans for the future, the seventeen-year-old feigned ignorance. Since he wasn't ready to tell his father about his musical aspirations, Enrique had no choice but to try to go along with his father's wishes, which were to attend a nearby college where he could keep an eye on him.

With almost no professional prospects to call his own, Enrique acquiesced to his father's demands. Yet the proud young man would not go so gently into that good lecture hall. Regardless of what his father wanted for him, Enrique's priorities would never change. If school prevented him from following his dream, he promised himself that he would quit right on the spot. In the meanwhile, he would work toward his business administration degree, while waiting for the musical break that would expedite his early departure.

Despite the piles of homework and barrage of early wake-up calls, attending the University of Miami served him well. It was there that he first began dating, making new friends, and coming into his own as an adult. Living under the shadow of his siblings and father had prevented Enrique from finding his own place in the world. Now that he was on his own at last, he was able to figure out what it was that he wanted out of life. And although he took advantage of everything college life had to offer, he never lost sight of his ultimate goal. Business courses were all well and good, but Enrique could not see himself wearing a suit and tie, and duking it out in the business arena for the rest of his life. He had bigger ideas for the future. Already three years into his studies, quitting school seemed completely out of the question. But that's exactly what Enrique decided to do. As he later recalled to the *Washington Post,* "I packed my bags and left, and said, 'If it goes well, it goes well. If it goes wrong, I have no one to blame.' "

Telling no one but his closest friends of the decision, Enrique carried on as always, pretending that he was still a student. His parents had absolutely no idea that their youngest son was being anything less than absolutely forthright. This secrecy, instead of alleviating the pressure to succeed in the music industry, served only to heighten the tension Enrique felt at striking out on his own. He figured that if he emerged victorious, with a record contract and a great album, his parents' pride would supplant their ire at his deceitfulness. If he failed miserably, however, Isabel and Julio would be doubly disappointed. Like it or not, Enrique had gotten himself into quite a predicament.

To give himself a fighting chance, he enlisted the aid of his father's manager, Fernan Martinez. At first the idea of confiding in someone so close to Julio seemed risky. But because Fernan and Enrique had grown close over the years, the young artist believed that his secret would not be compromised. Besides, Fernan was a very skilled manager. And earning his support could mean the difference between becoming a businessman and following his heart.

Upon hearing of Enrique's request for a private meeting, Fernan was curious to find out what the young man had on his mind. "My first reaction was: He's in trouble," Martinez told the *Washington Post*. "I thought it was something with a girl, he was so mysterious and secretive! I had no clue."

When Fernan and Enrique finally sat down together, the former was anxious to show the manager what he could do. As soon as he turned on his music, Enrique was automatically transported into a world of his own creation. He sang five songs, three of which were in English.

Watching the young man perform with all the maturity of a honed veteran, Fernan could see that Enrique had been busy. He had the grace, the sensuality, and lyrical resonance that was the mark of true musical greatness. And Fernan was in a position to know. He had been Julio's manager for the past nine years. "It was beautiful," he recalled, "the expression, the eyes, the hands, the body. You could see how much he believed in what he's singing."

Enrique had worked long and hard to be able to block out all distractions and transport himself into the moment so completely. His powers of concentration had been strengthened by repeated isolation, and, judging by Martinez's enthusiasm, Enrique was well on his way to reaping the rewards of these efforts.

Martinez thought that he and Enrique had a done deal, until he heard something that he couldn't believe—Enrique didn't want to use his real last name. The young singer was dead set on winning a record contract based solely on his own merits. While Enrique worried that record executives would give him preferential treatment because he was the son of a Latin music legend, Martinez was counting on that fact. No matter how convincing Enrique's explanations were, the manager could not fathom complicating an already difficult process.

"Why do you want to take the hard way?" asked Martinez. "We have the easiest way."

But Enrique wouldn't budge. Finally, Martinez relented, agreeing to help Enrique record a demo anyway. That done, he promised to shop it around to all the major label executives. The only hitch was that instead of reading Enrique Iglesias, the demo would bear the name "Enrique Martinez."

His manager could only shake his head and smile as if to say, "What's wrong with these kids today?" But for all of his apprehensions, Fernan Martinez made good on his promise. He spent hours hunting down major record company execs, duplicating Enrique's demo, and sending it off to the labels.

Although Enrique had not dared to anticipate a positive response, he was also unprepared for the slew of rejections that came wafting his way. He was dismayed to discover that all of the big labels, including Sony, EMI Latin, and PolyGram Latino, had turned him down. To add insult to injury, their rejections were all similarly misguided. " 'You're too young and you can't sing this kind of music, because people won't like this coming from a young guy.' I thought, 'What the hell are you talking about? OK, whatever.' "

In the mid-1990s, Latin artists were still extremely limited, with older singers being favored over new ones. The record companies and radio stations had no idea that younger audiences were clamoring for a new sound. Even though Enrique was still confident about bridging the age gap, he was beginning to feel the first pangs of heartbreak. All of the songs on his demo had been penned when he was in his mid-teens. If he'd been able to compose those mature sentiments at such a young age, then why should the companies refuse to sign him up?

"They always visualized a Spanish ballad singer

to be forty and up," Enrique explained to the *Buffalo News*. "When I was nineteen, they said, 'It doesn't work, no nineteen-year-olds do this; it's not possible.' I kept on believing in what I was doing. And I believed there was a younger audience for what I was doing. They said, 'There's no such thing as your kind of music sung by young guys.' "

Of course, the burgeoning singer would beg to differ. Besides his age, Enrique had yet another stumbling block tripping up his progress—the simplicity of his melodies and lyrics. For one reason or another, the standards held up for Latin music were not the same that existed for English-speaking artists. "What they didn't know is that simplicity is sometimes the best. I was used to American records, where the music was so simple, but so deep," opined Enrique. "Spanish record companies, they make music that is so complicated, with too many chords, too many changes, too many cheesy lyrics—instead of being direct and to the point."

Ironically enough, Julio Iglesias had hit upon a similar roadblock early on in his career. Like Enrique, the elder Iglesias had prided himself on keeping his music as uncomplicated as possible. "The lyrics are about simple, ordinary things, the stories between couples everywhere in the world," he informed a journalist. "It is a musical chat. Not intellectual. Not sophisticated. It's how people talk to each other when they are close."

At last, it seemed that Enrique and Julio actually had something in common. But whether Enrique knew that he and his father shared the same musical philosophy was uncertain. All he cared about was making music. And the thought of getting shut out of the music industry at such an early age was extremely disconcerting.

Just as he was about to lose all faith in the record labels, a glimmer of hope sprang into his heart. A small record label had received the demo, and were interested in meeting with the mysterious Enrique Martinez. "I got rejected by three record companies," he revealed to *Florida Today*, "and then this record company that I didn't know, Los Angeles–based Fonovisa Records, got back to me. They said, 'We like your music. We'd like to meet you.'"

Like fresh water to a dehydrated camel, those words reinvigorated Enrique's outlook on life. His previous rejections had rocked his confidence and blurred his bright vision of the future. Now, all that was forgotten. He had landed the offer that he had been waiting and preparing for all of his life. The elation he felt could not be described, but it was tempered by the fact that he couldn't share the good news with the people he loved most.

Enrique had to muster every ounce of restraint to keep the life-changing event under wraps. This was the best thing that had ever happened to him. Someone was actually interested in his music, and he was on top of the world. Like a ringing telephone, the words "They like, they like me, they like me" echoed through his mind.

He could not have hoped for a smoother contract negotiation process. Both Enrique and the staff at Fonovisa were extremely happy to be working together, and this mutual appreciation was felt by all. Enrique was extremely grateful to the up-and-coming label for taking a chance on an unknown singer. He was pleased that they'd chosen him for his music, not for being Julio Iglesias's son. In the end, Enrique's manager had succeeded in negotiating a three-album deal for a total of one million dollars. Although it was a tidy sum for a new artist, the young singer would have signed up for free if it meant that he could sing his music in front of a captivated audience.

Almost as if to reward the company for going out on a limb, Enrique decided to use his legal name to help market his work in progress. "I was like 'Somebody wants me, they like my music, screw it, let's just sign,' " he told MTV.

What had first seemed like a high-risk venture to the label turned out to be the best investment they ever made. The fact that the Fonovisa executives had had no idea that Enrique was Julio's son when they made him an offer gave them a profound sense of accomplishment. It was like finding a needle in a haystack. They had stumbled upon a potential gold mine, and were about to receive a major return on their investment. "Once I got signed, they knew who I was," he relayed to *Florida Today*. "But when we first talked about the deal, they didn't know my real name."

Making the decision to use his birth name hadn't been easy. Enrique thought long and hard about all the potential benefits and pitfalls that could arise. Comparisons and overly high expectations were only a few of the problems that Enrique foresaw in the future.

Aware of the press's ability to track down the facts, Enrique had no doubts that the sleuths would one day uncover the truth about his famous moniker. Besides, Enrique did not want to put up a false front to the world. He was, after all, an Iglesias. For better or worse, Enrique would always remain faithful to the people that brought him into this world. "That's part of my blood and heritage and who I am," he asserted to the *Calgary Sun*. "Even if I went by just my first name, you'd still ask about my dad and people would know who I am."

The media had been waiting for Enrique's story for as long as he'd been alive. Reporters were always snooping around, trying to probe into the personal lives of the Iglesias children. Enrique knew full well what a premature discovery of his plans could do to his career. Not only would it raise people's expectations, it would distract him from crafting his first album. The last thing he wanted now was for something to interfere with his artistic vision. Keeping his music pure and unfiltered was his top priority. And to ensure that he would have absolutely no resistance, from either his parents or the media, Enrique decided to record his eponymously titled debut album in Toronto, Canada.

Toronto was a place where Enrique could lose himself completely. Without all the familiar trappings of Miami to stunt his vision, the new surroundings stimulated his senses and liberated his mind. "I did the most important part there—the vocals. I wanted to get away, so I thought Canada would be the perfect place."

For the first time in his life, Enrique was completely on his own. All of the pressure, the secrecy, and anticipation he associated with Miami was suddenly lifted. Because Enrique valued the cathartic power of his music, he needed complete isolation. He wanted time to reflect and meditate so that his innermost feelings could be channeled into lyrics.

To his credit, Enrique had already written several quality songs when he was just a teenager. Instead of writing a whole new batch of compositions for the debut album, Enrique decided that his music should document the different stages of his life. And who better to express the pain and isolation of youth than the young boy who was there to experience it firsthand? Although Enrique would never forget the battle scars of adolescence, he was unable to express his feelings with the same clarity and poignancy that he'd captured at that age. "My first album, which was all Spanish, most of the songs I wrote in that album are like from when I was fifteen, sixteen," he told MTV.

Singing of loss and heartache, Enrique's lyrics were as fresh and uncomplicated as the face of a newborn infant. More importantly, they reflected the fears of abandonment that had plagued him since he was just a little boy. Songs like "*Si Tu Te Vas*" (If You Leave), "*Si Juras Regrasar*" (If You Swear to Return), "*Falta Tanto Amor*" (So Much Love Lost), and "*Muñeca Cruel*" (Cruel Doll) spoke of unrequited love and unfulfilled promises. There was no doubt that his upbringing had influenced the content of his lyrics. And even the newer songs reflected his repeated efforts to overcome past grievances and disappointments. "When I sing, mainly when I write a song if I do not feel it," he would later say, "I do not write it."

The struggles he'd had to overcome made for an unforgettable and universal sound. Hiding behind his music was impossible. If anything, composing music helped him come to terms with the demons that still plagued his soul. "I have always wanted to be a better artist than a great singer," he informed *La Opinion*. "There are a million good voices. For me, an artist is to be able to communicate, is able to tell a story. When I am singing a song I am telling my story. And to know how to give credibility to that story, and to know what I feel in my heart and that others feel it too, that is what I have always wanted."

Holed up in his hotel room in Toronto for over five months, Enrique had to work overtime to complete the songs for his first album. Whereas before he could let the story of his life unfold as it happened, he would now need to accelerate the verbalization of his most abstract thoughts. Quiet reflection and listening to soothing music helped Enrique complete the daunting task at hand.

The process of dredging up old wounds to produce the compelling songs had its repercussions. The young singer would often come out of his writing sessions drained and exhausted. He was by no means a seasoned songwriter. But whatever he lacked in the experience department, he made up threefold with piercing insight and raw honesty.

"Writing songs is very difficult for me," Enrique explained. "I am not a professional songwriter, I cannot write about a given subject, nor at any time I wish. It has to be something that has happened to me or which comes to me perhaps in a strange manner. And then I spend many hours revising what I have written, changing it until I arrive at the final result. There are many songs that die in the attempt."

Enrique's choice of words—"die"—couldn't be more telling. The completion of each song would herald a thousand metaphorical deaths and rebirths.

It was as if he were throwing off the shackles of the past, to emerge with renewed vigor and confidence. By the time *Enrique Iglesias* was finished, the boy had transformed himself into a man.

In order to reinforce his tranquil state of mind, Enrique opted to limit all of his songs to simple ballads. Instrumentally complex, fast-paced rock songs had their time and place, but they were useless in furthering his mission to introduce his real self to the world. The simplicity and emotion of ballads made them the ideal vehicles through which to launch his first album. "My influence was simple, straightforward music. When you can tell a story with 100 words, that's good. If you need 500 words, it's just more complicated. It was funny, but a lot of bands I listened to, whether it was Bruce Springsteen or Billy Joel, or Foreigner or Journey or the Police— these guys were rockers, but their biggest hits mainly were ballads—and simple, simple ballads, no more than three or four chords."

As soon as Enrique had selected the first single of his album, "*Si Tu Te Vas*," Fonovisa began an extensive radio campaign. At the time, radio DJs were infamous for their snubbing of new Latin singers, but once they heard Enrique's plaintive ballad, they were hooked.

Billed as just "Enrique," the label wanted to gauge their young artist's impact on audiences. At the time, few people knew that Enrique was actually the son of the famous Julio Iglesias. But that did nothing to deter them from calling in and requesting his single hour after hour. Once word had spread about the new balladeer, other radio stations got into the groove. Pretty soon, you couldn't turn on a Spanish radio station without hearing Enrique's soulful voice emanating from its airwaves.

Pleasing music listeners was one thing, but winning over music buyers was quite another. Unable to predict whether his album would sell, Enrique prayed for the best. Night after night, the young singer would lie awake, making desperate pleas for the realization of his dreams. It wasn't financial success that he was after so much as the recognition of the listeners. After all, he already had everything that money could buy. To gain the love of the people, however, Enrique would need talent.

On September 25, 1995, copies of his debut album were shipped to record stores around the world. Enrique's heart fluttered at the mere thought of music buyers listening to his album. Brought up to be a guarded and private person, Enrique knew that the release of his album would finally bring him out of his shell. People were becoming acquainted with a part of him that he had not even dared to reveal to his family. His days of loneliness and clandestine songwriting sessions were over. Millions of people were about to discover the true Enrique Iglesias.

The raw honesty of his lyrics and his heartfelt delivery caused an immediate stir. His single's wide radio airplay propelled a slew of anxious consumers into the stores. Music stores also displayed large posters with Enrique's album cover. From that point on, there would be no mistaking the fact that he was indeed Julio Iglesias's son.

Because the incredible radio response had proven once and for all that he had what it took to succeed on his own, the young singer approved the use of his full name on his album's cover art. He would no longer harbor worries about riding on his father's far-reaching coattails.

The incredible success of the album in the first few weeks of its release demanded that Enrique come clean with his family. News of his album was just beginning to spread, and with all the offers for interviews, magazine covers, and television spots pouring in each day, Enrique knew that he could not keep his secret for long.

He could not stomach the thought of his parents finding out about his new album from a secondary source. Whatever issues he'd had with Isabel and Julio, they did not absolve him of his responsibilities. He would have to find a way to break the news, and fast.

Enrique had anticipated the dreaded moment from the very first time he put pen to paper. But he was no longer the same shy, insecure young boy of yesteryear. He had become a responsible young man with a successful music career. For all of his professional coups, however, Enrique still turned into a little boy whenever his father entered the room. His sense of parental authority and fear would not disappear overnight.

To avoid making a scene, Enrique opted to tell his father about his new album at a large party held by a family friend. The young singer watched his father out of the corner of his eye, waiting for the perfect moment to pounce. But just as Enrique began to think that Julio would never stop making the rounds and socializing with the bevy of admirers gathering beside him, his father approached him for an informal tête-à-tête. It was then that Enrique finally told his dad about everything. From quitting school to being signed by Fonovisa to recording in Toronto. The torrent of words poured forth fast and furious. Enrique held nothing back.

As he unraveled the tale, Julio's face betrayed his true feelings of distress. He could not hide his disappointment at not having been consulted. On the other hand, he was flattered to discover that Enrique had been carving out a life path similar to his own. In a nutshell, Julio's ego was doing battle with itself. "My father and I spoke after he found out, and he was shocked," Enrique told *People*. "I said, 'Look, this is exactly what I've always wanted to do. Just let me do it my way, please.'"

Doing it *his* way would become a recurring theme in the young singer's life. But the need for independence became even more pronounced when Julio began advising Enrique on how to run his career. After finding himself so completely out of the loop, Julio's immediate reaction was to make up for lost time. With his wealth of knowledge of all the ins and outs of the music business, Julio felt that Enrique could go very far indeed. The problem was that his son's days of longing for parental advice were now long gone.

As stubborn as he might have seemed to most outsiders, Enrique felt certain that controlling his own career was in everyone's best interest. Recalling the strained relationship that had developed between his father and his uncle Carlos when the two first tried working together, Enrique feared that his own relationship with Julio would suffer the same fate. To sidestep any potential resentments or ill will, Enrique responded to his father's offers with an unequivocal, "Thank you, but no thank you."

The fifty-year-old singer could not believe his ears. Having sold 200 million records worldwide, Julio was the ultimate role model for dozens of Latin singers. Any one of them would have traded their right arm for his input, and here was his son refusing his counsel. There was no doubt that Julio was hurt by Enrique's do-it-yourself attitude, but he kept his feelings to himself. "But I will be happy for Enrique, if his singing career is successful," Julio informed the Gannett News Service. "I told him to do as he wishes, but do it well because this is something very serious. I'm trying to work with him . . . advise him on things such as accepting offers too quickly. But he's listening with a deaf ear."

To condemn Enrique's refusal to collaborate with his father would be unfair. He was, after all, a fiercely independent young man with very clear ideas about the direction of his life. Besides, Julio was known for being somewhat of a know-it-all. "He thinks he knows everything," Chabeli told *People*. "I am the only person in his world who will tell him I don't think he's right. Sometimes I think he would rather I shut up!"

Few people aside from his children had ever had the nerve to stand up to the awe-inspiring signer. Julio's lifestyle had instilled Enrique with the very independence he was now urging him to sacrifice. Of course, Enrique was adamant about retaining full control. "They were surprised, but they understood my position," Enrique conveyed to the *Chicago Sun-Times*. "It's not a matter of being supportive or not. I was going to do it anyway, I have always been independent about the choices in my life."

After coming clean with his father, Enrique made haste to brief his mother on all the latest developments. Like her ex-husband, Isabel was completely unprepared for the subject of her talk with Enrique. As far as she knew, he was still studying business administration at the University of Miami. As she found out, Enrique had not only left school without informing her, but he was planning to become a singer. Crossing herself, Isabel immediately prayed for her son's well-being.

Having lived with an international singing sensation, Isabel knew that Enrique's career choice would be both a blessing and a curse. After enduring her father-in-law's kidnapping and worrying about the safety of her own children, the last thing she wanted was added exposure for Enrique. It was bad enough that her daughter had become such a high-profile model and actress. Now her youngest son was planning to go public with his new album. Suffice it to say that at first Isabel was not at all thrilled by the prospect. "I think my mother . . . she was a little worried," Enrique told MTV.

But time would allay her fears. Once she had unearthed all the glorious details of Enrique's short career, Isabel expressed her enthusiasm and happiness openly. A mother's pride has no bounds, and Isabel wasted no time before spreading the news about her now-famous son.

For all of his mother's PR efforts on his behalf, Enrique fared very well on his own. On November 6, 1995, "*Si Tu Te Vas*" showed up at number six on the *Billboard* Latin charts. Only a few weeks later, the single soared even higher, landing squarely in the number one position. The second single released from the debut, "*Experiencia Religiosa*," also fared well on the charts, reaching the number three position only days after its release. Given the artist's newcomer status, his success was truly astounding. But then again, Enrique was an exceptional singer with an uncommon gift.

With his debut album also climbing the charts and hitting the number three position, Enrique knew it was time to begin a massive publicity campaign. He had been in hiding long enough. He would need to make plenty of appearances to keep his new fans satisfied.

Working in association with Fonovisa and his manager Martinez, Enrique's new publicity person booked Enrique on every radio show and television program that would have him. Then, it was on to a full tour of record stores around the world. At one promotion party held in Los Angeles, Enrique got his first taste of life in the celebrity lane. Three thousand young girls had showed up to meet and greet the youngest Iglesias crooner. His arrival caused such a panic that security personnel were called in to safely escort the dazed and confused singer through the crowd of onlookers.

More national coverage came in the form of a guest spot on NBC's *Hard Copy*. Millions of women, who had seen the young singer on TV, were flooding Fonovisa with phone calls. Proposals of marriage, letters of gratitude, and words of praise poured into Enrique's already growing fan file. Short of rolling around in ecstasy in his huge pile of fan mail, the young singer could find no way to express his happiness. The fans had finally embraced him, and they have yet to let go.

However, the thrill of the media joyride would not last forever. At the very beginning of his career, Enrique learned a valuable lesson about the dangers of overexposure. Besides the constant allusions to his famous father, Enrique was often accused of having relied on his father for everything from vocal training to business management. While a less proud and independent man might have let these biting comments slide, Enrique was not about to let the press have the last word.

Enrique loved to do television interviews. He felt that the medium brought him face-to-face with his fans, while allowing his music to gain the maximum exposure. But on one occasion, appearing on a television show proved anything but pleasant. Just as Enrique had prepped himself for what he thought would surely be an exciting experience, he heard his introduction through the green room speaker. Instead of highlighting all of his recent accomplishments, the reporter introduced him only as the "son of Julio Iglesias." A few seconds passed in which Enrique contemplated ignoring the ill-mannered greeting. But the longer he thought about it, the more convinced he became that it was time to leave. Without a word to anyone but his manager, Enrique calmly strolled out of the production studio never to return again.

This incident is telling for several reasons. Being Julio Iglesias's son was an important part of Enrique's self-concept. But there were many other sides to him that were just as vital. All Enrique wanted was to be treated like a person, a whole person. The media's attempt to detract from his dynamic persona only intensified his determination to overcome the supposed privileges of being born an Iglesias.

Also important was Enrique's refusal to compromise when it came to his career. Choosing to take on all the responsibility for his failures and his successes was brave. But it also made him feel extremely vulnerable. And when someone threatened his career, he became even more resolute in defending his position. "When it comes down to my music," Enrique informed MTV, "I've always said, 'It's my career. If I screw it up, I'm the one who's screwed.' So I don't want anyone else to screw it up."

Fortunately for the intense young man, he would not have to live under his father's shadow much longer. When *Enrique Iglesias* first debuted, Julio's single "*Baila Morena*," from his new album *La Carretera*, was also just beginning to make the rounds. The media had a blast writing about the parallel careers of father and son, but the fun would be short-lived. While Enrique's first single skyrocketed to the number one position, his father's single, which peaked at number twelve, fell off the *Billboard* chart entirely. Still, radio stations interested in a good family saga played Enrique's and Julio's music back-to-back.

Father and son were no doubt disturbed by all the comparisons. After all, each had a solo act with no intentions of expanding in the near future. "Radio stations worldwide are playing Julio's and Enrique's singles back-to-back," Sandy Miller, a spokeswoman for Fonovisa International in Miami, told the Gannett News Service.

No matter how much the press would try to pit

father and son against one another, both Enrique and Julio avoided discussing each other's musical careers. In fact, it seemed that Julio had suddenly become reconciled to aging gracefully. But whether that had anything to do with Enrique's sudden visibility would never be determined. "I look in the mirror now and see age is coming," explained Julio. "There's more wrinkles. People can't say I'm a sexy guy anymore. That makes me happy because now I know I have fans because of something else."

When the press discovered that the two singers were not about to engage in any public displays of competition, they began speculating about the possibility of future collaborations.

Reporters would grill Enrique, asking, "Is there any chance you and your father will record a duet anytime soon?"

Much to their dismay, the answer would always be "No."

As much as Enrique respected Julio's music, he wasn't about to put on a great show of affection for the benefit of the entertainment press corps. As far as Enrique was concerned, there would be no teary-eyed duets and staged bear hugs for the paparazzi to feed on.

Julio was also dead-set against singing with Enrique. Of course, Enrique's curt dismissal of the subject may have had something to do with his father's attitude. But, be that as it may, Julio made it clear that he was by no means jumping at the chance to collaborate with his son. "I don't want to sing with Enrique right now," said Julio. "He's very young and he has a lot to learn. But I would like to perform with him in a few years."

Enrique did have a lot to learn about the music industry, but he also had plenty of important lessons to impart. In the following year, his album would sell over five million copies. And while record sales are not an indication of acquired wisdom, it was a sign that Enrique would never have to labor under the weight of his father's name again. When he walked into a room, people would finally say, "There goes Enrique" instead of "There goes Julio's son." And for now, that was all the confirmation Enrique needed.

SIX

Rising to the Challenge

With the Rocky theme song ringing in his ears, Enrique felt as if he had really overcome all obstacles. His album was flying high in *Billboard*'s number one position, his label was clamoring for a follow-up album, and Enrique himself was scheduled to launch a worldwide tour with the release of his second album. The future had platinum written all over it.

Before the release of his debut album, Enrique's main concern had been to rise to the uppermost ranks of the music industry. Now that he'd scaled those lofty heights, all he had to do was figure out how to stay there. As any one-hit wonder can attest, getting to the top is one thing, but keeping your audience interested is another matter altogether. Enrique knew that his next album would have to surpass all expectations. Music critics were just waiting to tear into his sophomore effort. For whatever reason—his age, his family connection—most critics believed that the singer just didn't have what it took to craft another hit.

But Enrique did not get to number one by doubting his abilities. All he needed was time alone to compose new material. But securing a schedule that would allow him to pen his famous hits was easier said than done. Whereas Enrique had had his whole life to come up with the songs on his first album, his follow-up would have to be the product of one long, concentrated effort. Of course, with his obligations to the press and to the audience mounting with each passing week, Enrique realized that he'd only have a few hours a day to devote to the all-important sophomore album. "I need to be at home, sleeping there at least two weeks or even more and just writing in my room," he told MTV. "That's where I write. Late at night in my room, when everyone is sleeping, from, like, two in the morning 'til eight o'clock in the morning."

Even though Enrique had finally come out of hiding, he still needed that seclusion and secrecy in order to write with conviction. Enrique had access to any studio in the world, but inspiration could only find him when he was in a room of his own. That's how he first began to write, and that's how he's continued to churn out hits ever since.

Unwilling to mess with a tried-and-true formula, Enrique decided that his next album, entitled *Vivir* (To Live), would also concentrate on ballads. Not only was he a skilled balladeer, but, like his father, he was most comfortable singing simple songs with simple messages. However, he also wanted to spice up the mix with a smattering of pop sounds and rhythms. His fans would be expecting an even bigger production, and the last thing he wanted was to disappoint them.

Little did he know that *Vivir* would mark a major artistic transition in his career. The maturity he had gained since *Enrique Iglesias* first came out was evident in everything from the profound lyrics to the professional production. He had grown considerably since he first began writing, and was becoming more skilled in conveying his innermost thoughts and feelings.

Vivir was slated to be an even more personal and self-aware album. Taking over ten months to produce, the follow-up would take risks that its predecessor had not. Emboldened by his first effort, Enrique pulled out all the stops, allowing the audience a rare glimpse into his mind and heart. "It's more intimate," said Enrique. "It took ten months to finish and I am more satisfied with it."

On January 29, 1997, the world was introduced to a smarter and more confident Enrique. *Vivir* had not only matched his first album's level of intensity, but it surpassed it musically. Critics who praised his first album for its sincerity, were now heaping even more accolades on the young singer. "You'll be hard-pressed to find a better new pop album than *Vivir* (To Live)," wrote one critic. "Sung entirely in Spanish, it is filled with catchy, well-produced songs you'll find yourself humming after the first playing. Iglesias cowrote the bulk of the songs . . . and he's upped the tempos, slipping biting guitar solos into power-pop ballads such as "*Al Despertar*" (Waking Up), "*Enamorado Por Primera Vez*" (In Love for the First Time), and the terrific "*Miente*" (Lie).

A music critic from the *Dallas Morning News*

wrote, " '*Lluvia Cae*,' with its chant intro and effervescent, reggae-tinged beat, is a bouncy good time. '*Solo En Ti*' (Only You), a Spanish version of British electronic duo Yaz's 1982 single, is an expertly arranged, textured pop song. '*Al Despertar*,' featuring fine instrumental work by bassist Leland Sklar, guitarist Michael Landau, and drummer Greg Bissonette, simmers in a sexy, rhythmic vibe accentuated by Mr. Iglesias's powder-keg delivery."

While positive musical reviews warmed his heart, Enrique refused to pay too much attention to the press. In fact, he was his own harshest critic. Getting the best work out of himself had always been his sole motivation. And while he was pleased with his first album, he was utterly elated with the results of his second effort.

His label also anticipated great things the second time around. Since his first album had sold over five million albums, the label was ready and waiting to distribute three million copies all over the world. And when *Vivir* finally hit the stores, Fonovisa was actually forced to make another shipment of two million copies. *Vivir* sold a grand total of five million copies throughout South and Central America, Europe, and even Asia in its first week.

Enrique accomplished the unthinkable. Never before had a Latin artist sold so many albums in so little time. But this was not to be the only record set by Enrique Iglesias. He quickly set another when his album went platinum in Taiwan, something no Latin artist had ever been able to achieve. "It sold because a Chinese artist recorded two of my songs in Chinese," Enrique tried to play down his accomplishment in the *Washington Post*. "And it doesn't sound that bad!"

Enrique was outselling Latin singers left and right. No one could compete with his phenomenal success, not even his father. Having just released his latest effort, called *Tango*, Julio Iglesias was expecting his own share of critical acclaim and attention. Imagine his surprise when he discovered that his youngest son's album was selling twice as fast as his own.

Enrique was doubly honored when he got the nod for a Grammy nomination in the Best Latin Pop Performance category. Enrique had won many awards including several *Billboard* awards, seven Premios Lo Nuestro, and two ASCAP awards for Best Composer, but the Grammys were the ultimate in musical recognition.

When Enrique received the nomination, he found out that the award was by no means a done deal. He was up against some pretty stiff competition, including Luis Miguel, Jose Feliciano, Marco Antonio Solís, and Viki Carr. But the illustrious names could only add to his enthusiasm. The nomination meant that Enrique was not only accepted by the fans, but by the music industry as well.

Sharing the news with his parents and siblings was one of the happiest moments of his life. And when his family discovered that Enrique was being nominated for the same award that Julio had been nominated for the previous year, they were duly thrilled. Chabeli and Julio Jr. were especially impressed with how far Enrique had come. Whereas before they would tease and torment him, they now looked upon him with admiration. Wishing him nothing but the best of luck, the entire Iglesias clan prepared to sit in anticipation until the award show.

Although his family had no doubt that he would walk away a winner, Enrique was not so sure. Many music experts had put their money on Luis Miguel. Ever the humble novice, Enrique was inclined to agree with them.

February 26, 1997, was a day that would remain etched in Enrique's memory forever. He, along with the rest of the nominees, had gotten up early to prepare for the big day. Enrique was actually relieved that he was not favored to win, since it alleviated much of the pressure that went hand in hand with the Grammys. Still, Enrique wanted to look and feel his best for the big day. The Grammys would be broadcast around the world, drawing an audience that exceeded 1.5 billion. This was the day he had been waiting for.

While one part of him savored the excitement of the proceedings, another part criticized all the pomp and circumstance. Having to dress up, ride in a limousine, and smile for the cameras had become second nature for him. But there was still a side of him that wanted to play the Latin bad boy, and show up at the ceremony with torn jeans, a T-shirt, and a devil-may-care attitude.

Enrique refused to get caught up in the moment. Maintaining perspective and keeping his priorities straight was extremely important to him. After all, it wasn't as if he'd started writing music just so he could have a Grammy to display on his mantel. "If they give the prize to me, I will feel very grateful, as I feel now by the nomination," he confessed to the Associated Press. "But if it does not happen, it will not change anything, since my greater challenge is to continue singing."

Still, Enrique knew full well how much was riding on the ceremony. Everyone, from his record label to his family to his manager, was counting on him to make a great first impression. And that is all he intended to do when he arrived at the large orchestra hall.

As laid back as he tried to be, the excitement and thrill of being nominated eventually took its toll. No sooner had Enrique arrived than he began to feel queasy and unsettled. The pressure had apparently gotten to the cool customer, and he had no choice but to take refuge for an hour or so.

When he finally did make an appearance, Enrique felt better than ever. He scanned the room looking for a familiar face. But everyone he saw was familiar in one way or another. Whether he had watched them on TV, attended their concerts, or listened to their music as a young boy, all of Enrique's music idols had gathered underneath one roof. The crème de la crème had come out to celebrate the music industry's biggest night, and Enrique was there to see it all.

As he walked through the room completely starstruck and amazed, he felt just like the boy who'd stammered upon meeting Michael Jackson for the first time. "I was only twenty-one," he reported to MTV. "It was a great feeling. Just to be surrounded by so many great singers, so many great artists, felt very good."

The young singer couldn't believe that he was in the midst of all these phenomenal talents. What made the experience even more incredible was that

Enrique in concert.

(©Nina Azzarone, Karen Labs, NY)

Belting out one of his famous love songs.

(© Nina Azzarone, Karen Labs, NY)

Always gracious, he pauses to thank the fans.

(© Nina Azzarone, Karen Labs, NY)

His concerts are always exciting.

(© Nina Azzarone, Karen Labs, NY)

At a Los Angeles festival.

(© Albert L. Ortega, MH Photos)

Fans are always delighted to meet the sexy singer.

(© Albert L. Ortega, MH Photos)

Proud Enrique with his American Music Award.

(© Albert L. Ortega)

Enrique takes a break in the midst of a whirlwind tour.

(© Corbis/Mitch Gerber)

he had become one of them. It finally dawned on Enrique that he was no longer on the outside looking in, a realization that wouldn't truly hit home until later on that evening.

When the lights began to blink and the myriad of well-dressed and impeccably groomed celebrities filed into the main hall, Enrique was quick to take his seat. He was anxious to enjoy the festivities, and see the many talented acts scheduled to perform that evening. After his initial sickness had subsided, Enrique decided that he would just try to have a good time and not think about the outcome of the award show.

Enrique enjoyed himself so much that he completely lost sight of the fact that his category for Best Latin Pop Performance was coming up. That is, until he heard his name being announced as one of the nominees. Suddenly, he felt the full weight of his desire for the coveted Grammy. There was no denying that he wanted that trophy—bad.

"And the winner is . . ."

The presenter fumbled with the envelope.

"Enrique Iglesias!"

Enrique could barely hear his name above the screams of the fans and the clapping of industry insiders. He asked himself, "Have I really won? Could this be a joke or a dream?" Well, there was only one way to find out. With his vision blurred by tears of joy, Enrique tried to make his way toward the podium. As he stood there surveying the crowd, he knew he was obligated to say thank you. But just before he opened his mouth, he stopped for a moment and took a deep breath. "Thank you God," he spoke inwardly. "Thank you God!"

*   *   *

The euphoria of that moment was like nothing Enrique had ever experienced. Holding on to his Grammy as if it were an anchor, Enrique sailed through the rest of the night's responsibilities as if in a daze. Holding court at the head of the press room, posing for dozens of pictures with fellow winners, attending the after-hours celebrations . . . the evening was a mad whirlwind of activity. It was only much later, when Enrique had time to reflect, that he was finally able to make sense of all that had transpired.

Winning the Grammy award put him front and center before an audience of 1.5 billion people. His albums had been selling out, but the award show accelerated their already mind-boggling sales rate. Although industry veterans like to exaggerate the effects of the Grammys on an artist's career, Enrique realized that nothing had really changed. He would still have to work hard on making music, and never settle for anything but the absolute best. "I don't think because you win a Grammy, your career is made," he would later explain to MTV. "I mean, don't get me wrong, I'd rather win it than not get it, but it doesn't mean your career is made."

Having earned the coveted Grammy, the young man could have easily been carried away by his own hype. Everyone from publicists to his manager were telling him just how monumental his victory had been. But even though he secretly smiled every time he thought of that fateful evening, Enrique was determined to concentrate on what was really important—the quality of his music, the longevity of his career, and the satisfaction of his fans.

The three years Enrique spent studying business administration had not gone to waste. He had become a shrewd businessman. Nothing escaped his notice. Whether it was his accounts, his distribution, or tallying his sales, Enrique wanted to be involved in every aspect of his career. If anything needed to be done, Enrique was prepared to do it. And his next step would be to go on a worldwide promotional tour in support of *Vivir*.

The people had spoken. Judging by the thousands of letters he received each week, his fans were dying to see the young singer in the flesh. As Enrique could think of nothing more important than pleasing his loyal supporters, he made immediate preparations for his first tour.

Even though he had already shifted 12 million units of his two albums, Enrique had yet to step upon a stage. A nerve-racking experience for any untried live performer, the first tour promised to be anything but boring. Enrique's course of action was simple. In a few short weeks he would have to transform himself into the consummate entertainer, the kind of singer who feels just as comfortable on stage as he does in his bathroom shower.

Adding even more anxiety to the mix was the fact that his concert was selling out faster than anyone could have predicted. With over sixty-seven concerts scheduled all over the world, from the United States to Europe to Latin America, the *Vivir* tour would have to defy all expectations. No expense could be spared. This was the biggest coming-out party ever launched for any Latin artist, and Enrique was determined to make every show an unforgettable event.

"When I attended rock concerts in the United States, I would dream of being on one of those huge stages, full of magical lights and impressive sound," he stated in a press release. "Now I have the responsibility of presenting myself in front of an audience in a presentation which contains the best musicians and technicians. For this reason, we have invested everything possible to obtain the best all around and I think we have achieved it. I hope that the audience really enjoys the show to which I have put all of our souls into."

Preparing for the tour would be one of the most grueling experiences of his life. Enrique was ruthless in his determination to make his tour an exciting and action-packed extravaganza. It was, he figured, the least he could do for the fans who had turned him into an international star.

The singer would not leave anything to chance. Whether it was lighting, set construction, wardrobe, or sound, he made sure that every last aspect of his performance was held up to the highest standard. Another element that was of the utmost importance was the musicians that would accompany Enrique. He was determined to find the most talented and hardworking group available. Toward this end, he launched a long and arduous selection process that would last for several weeks.

With 150,000 pounds of set materials, including lights, sound, and other equipment, the production team rented eight large trucks and two C–130 airplanes to transport Enrique's gear. Besides all the equipment, the Enrique Iglesias entourage would include more than 65 employees, including technicians, production people, and musicians.

Everything had to be perfect. From the first day that his label announced the tour, fans had been queuing up at ticket counters, anxious to see Enrique perform live in concert. Enrique's tickets were going so fast that he even needed to add additional concert dates to such cities as New York, Los Angeles, and Chicago. Quite a coup considering the fact that every one of Enrique's concert venues had a capacity of no less than 12,000.

In Mexico, Enrique earned the esteemed right to perform in the world-famous bullfighting plaza, Plaza de Toros. With a capacity of 35,000, the arena was far too large for most Latin artists to fill. Enrique was the exception. Not only did he sell out the venue, but he managed to repeat the performance three nights in a row.

But Mexico would not be the only place where people would flock to see Enrique Iglesias. With two scheduled concerts and 65,000 tickets sold, Buenos Aires, Argentina, also proved to be fruitful ground for Enrique's showstopping act. "I'm playing big arenas because I can fill them up," he expressed. "Maybe next year I won't be able to. So I'm doing it now. That's the whole point of life: Seize the moment."

Selling out arenas and amphitheaters may have proved to be much easier than Enrique had anticipated, but he was still determined to give his fans their money's worth. With eighteen songs selected from his repertoire of hits—including *"Si Tu Te Vas," "Experiencia Religiosa," "Por Amarte," "No Llares Por Mi," "Trapecista,"* and *"Muneca Cruel"*— the concert would be a long one with plenty of special effects to keep the fans' eyes just as enthralled as their ears. The art of magic figured prominently into the spectacle, with Enrique slated to pull a vanishing act mid-concert. Another optical illusion involved an effect that required Enrique to ride atop a crane, high above the spectators' heads. When asked about the measure of difficulty involved in the death-defying act, Enrique responded to *USA Weekend*, "If I have to die, I'd love to die in concert. I'd die happy."

SEVEN

Around the World and Back

Cheering fans, their hearts aflutter, wait patiently for the arrival of their beloved balladeer. As the lights dim, Enrique Iglesias glides onto the stage. In the darkness, the audience can barely make him out. They see nothing except the silhouette of his well-toned physique. In less than a moment, Enrique's famous voice will pierce the stillness. But wait, what is he doing? As he stands in his typical "behold a living legend" posture, wearing his stage costume of tight jeans, white T-shirt, and billowing shirt, the light suddenly illuminates his face. Instead of striking the audience with his most smoldering of gazes, the singer surprises all by breaking into good-natured laughter. It is as if he is laughing at both himself and the concertgoers. He laughs as if to say, "Let's leave all our inhibitions and expectations at the door, and just have a good time." And for Enrique, that's what putting on a good show is all about.

Enrique's concert experience is unlike any other. It is like having an intimate conversation with a best friend or a lover. Generous, energetic, and intensely emotional night after showstopping night, Enrique sacrifices himself for the greater good of the audience. And even though thousands of women, all equally enraptured with the performer, come out to witness the spectacle, every last one walks away feeling as if she's just spent two hours listening to Enrique's private serenade.

As we gaze at Enrique's flawless live rendition of his greatest hits, it seems as if he has been doing it all of his life. His gracious manner and natural way of communicating with the audience make the job of entertaining 12,000 people night after night look effortless. But looks can be deceiving, because there is nothing easy or relaxing about touring for months at a time.

Life on the *Vivir* tour was hardly a cakewalk. The appreciation of his vociferous fanbase may have motivated Enrique to carry on, but there were times when the singer actually considered packing up and going home. There were many days when nothing seemed to be going right. And when you're on a full-scale, worldwide tour, those days are usually more the rule than the exception. Whether his sound system went awry or his lighting person had fallen ill, something would inevitably go wrong.

Technical glitches may have thrown Enrique off from time to time, but preserving his peace of mind and keeping his vocals tuned were his two main priorities. If Enrique hoped to keep his audience coming back night after passionate night, he would need to keep his voice in top-notch condition. But using his vocal chords on a daily basis was the very thing that could jeopardize his instrument. Fortunately, Enrique came up with a foolproof formula for battling a sore throat. "Eat a lot of pizza," Enrique stated with a straight face. "When your mouth is full, you don't talk as much; your voice doesn't get tired."

Devouring all that pizza *and* maintaining a washboard stomach? Now, who would believe something like that? But there he was, looking better than ever. Enrique's well-toned body was almost as important to the fans as his resonant vocals, and the fact that he wasn't embarrassed to show it all off during his shows didn't hurt either. Carried away by the emotion of his lyrics, Enrique would stretch and pull at his already torn T-shirt, making all the girls scream in the process. At one time, he might have been mortified at the thought of flaunting so much skin, but as his career progressed, Enrique realized that being a good showman meant making compromises.

The voice, the penetrating stare, the haunting lyrics . . . all of these elements combined to ignite the flame of his fans' desire. By the time Enrique had completed his set, his female fans were so hot and bothered that they often rushed the stage. At one concert, attended by over 14,000 people, the girls went mad with desire and tried to push themselves toward Enrique. Security guards were immediately put to work, linking their arms in a makeshift chain to deter the path of the stampeding girls. The scene was so incredible that Enrique felt as if he was back in Spain and running with the bulls in Pamplona. Nothing could stop the concertgoers in their tracks. All Enrique could do was hope for the best and try to stay out of their way.

There were other times when it seemed that Enrique underestimated the extent of his musical prowess, wreaking great havoc in his wake. "In Argentina, I threw out my pants and shirt, and people got hurt and trampled," he explained. "It was crazy. I'll never do that again."

Trying to sing above the din of the crowd was also a major hurdle for the young artist. Concert reviewers who came to appraise his showmanship always complained about not being able to hear the music. But Enrique took his fans' enthusiasm as just another sign that he was on the right track. "I've had a lot of critics say you know you can't go to an Enrique Iglesias concert because you don't hear the music, there's too much screaming going on," he told *Entertainment Weekly*. "I don't care. They can scream all they want. You know, I'm going to miss it when I'm fifty years old and they're not there."

Enrique knew when he was outnumbered. And since his booming tenor was no match for thousands of crazed young fans, Enrique could never resist a one-on-one meeting. One of the most exciting and highly anticipated moments of his concert was when Enrique scanned the audience, looking for the one lucky girl to serenade. Alone in their rooms, Enrique's fans would dream about a day when they'd be invited onto his stage. For many, this was the hope that kept them coming back night after night, and year after year.

Enrique's close encounters of the fan kind always included a personal serenade and a tender embrace. Those young ladies fortunate enough to be chosen would cry openly, as the young singer stroked their hair and kissed their faces. While such intimate contact with fans is usually reserved for the backstage, Enrique was not one to hide his emotions from the world. If he wanted to serenade a pretty girl, then he would do just that. Unfortunately for most of his fans, there was only so much of Enrique to go around.

Always on the lookout for attention-grabbing headlines, music critics tried to figure out just what it was that made Enrique such a hot commodity. There were all the obvious explanations: he had a good voice, a good body, and a charming smile. But so did many other performers. Enrique, however, never questioned the source of his mass appeal, telling *USA Today*, "It's completely sincere. Not only the lyrics and the music, but the singer. It's real. I will never sing a song I don't feel. I will never write a song that doesn't have to do with me. That's something you can't fake. You can fool one person, but you can't fool ten million people."

While some performers seek refuge from their fans behind the bulky frames of their security guards, Enrique prefers to do just the opposite. The young singer is unique in his desire to reach out to grasping fans, and allow them to touch, feel, and hug him. Reinforcing Enrique's full-body contact approach is his firm belief that the fans are there to protect him. The sight of a group of frantic girls may send some pop icons running for the hills, but Enrique just stands there, letting the love of his fans wash over him. "It's great, I mean, that's what makes it so good. I feel very protected when I'm around them."

Actually, Enrique's behavior is not all surprising. When you stop to consider that for many years Enrique didn't feel loved or appreciated, it makes perfect sense that he would embrace the fans who worship him from head to toe. The novelty of being the source of so much unbridled affection has yet to wear off.

Instead of protecting himself from his fans, Enrique often finds himself in the difficult position of having to shield his fans from the concert bodyguards. On one occasion, when security personnel came to remove a girl from the stage, Enrique took matters into his own hands and gently glided her off the stage while hugging her. "People jump on the stage all the time. It's like being with Elvis in Latin America'," explained a close friend and production manager. "But if somebody comes on and he sees a security guard trying to manhandle them or something, he'll instantly say, 'It's okay, it's okay.' And he'll let them come onstage. And you know they'll spend like twenty seconds and he'll, while he's singing, personally escort them off the side of the stage."

Conflict between Enrique and the security team is always ready to erupt—especially when the security guards realize that not only do they have to keep the fans away from Enrique, but that Enrique has to be kept away from the fans. Never before has a performer showed so much love and appreciation for his supporters. Sure, there are plenty of artists who make a concerted effort to thank the "little people," but their actions tell a different story. Enrique is one artist whose actions speak as loud, if not louder, than his words. When *La Opinion* asked about his unconventional rapport with his fans, Enrique responded, "But what damage can children like them do? Please, they are not going to do anything to me."

Enrique's unique way of handling his fans is just another indication of his tendency to always take the road less traveled. His enduring appeal might have been ignited by his sexy looks and passionate lyrics, but it is his personal style that keeps his fans loyal through thick and thin. As one excited fan gushed, Enrique is "like a down-to-earth type, like the boy next door that all the girls fall in love with."

Instead of being just another image crafted strategically for publicity purposes, Enrique's boy-next-door persona was as real as it gets. His nonchalant approach to fame had nothing to do with trying to appear above it all, but was instead a natural reaction to having grown up as Julio Iglesias's son. Because he always had more fame and money than he knew what to do with, Enrique never cared about the trappings of celebrity. Jets, limousines, and boats were just so much wasted metal. Having a good time meant doing regular things like eating McDonald's, watching sports, and waterskiing.

To this day, Enrique tries to leave the money matters to his financial managers. He worries that placing too much importance on wealth will prevent him from fully exploring his creativity, and rightly so. "I do not spend too much," he confided in *Gente*. "I walk around all the day in a T-shirt, jeans, and eight dollars in my pocket. They do not interest me, the private airplanes nor the properties. What I win I put it in the bank and it's just there."

Staying grounded amidst the many perks of fame—including women, mass adulation, and hobnobbing with the rich and famous—cannot be easy for anyone. Yet Enrique always kept things in perspective. Unlike the many young performers who rise too fast only to get swallowed by drug and alcohol abuse, Enrique was well aware of the delicate balance he'd have to strike to walk the tightrope of fame. Growing up with Julio Iglesias for a father had taught him everything he needed to know. "I don't really care about the . . . [expletive] of the music business," he asserted to the *Dallas Morning News*. "I got used to it because of my dad. It's not a matter of money. I've seen money my whole life. It's not a matter of fame. I've seen fame my whole life. . . . So, suddenly, when you have it yourself, you don't really care about it."

Still, Enrique had to make concerted efforts to keep from yielding to fame's innumerable temptations. Having seen one too many real-life *Behind the Music* episodes, Enrique never wanted to be just another music industry casualty. "If you get a kid who's twenty-two years old and has never seen any of this—selling millions of records, making a lot of money, having many women around him—it can definitely cause negative problems, and that's completely logical," he told the *Washington Post*. "Where this job affects you most is mentally. It can really screw you up—it takes away reality from you so fast."

Even though millions of women would have sold their souls for just one date with the young singer, Enrique could never understand what all the hoopla was about. When he looks at himself in the mirror, all he can see is an insecure young man with big ambitions. Never once does the word "star" or "heartthrob" enter his mind. After all, it wasn't so long ago that he was striking out with all the girls in high school.

Seemingly overnight, the media had decided to

turn him into a sex symbol by playing up his good looks and seductive personality. But all Enrique could think about was the awkward stage that he had gone through as a young boy. The thought that he was considered handsome only because he was famous often crossed his mind. "When I used to go to college, people did not see me as a sex symbol," he admitted. "I think I'm considered one now because of my music, but I know I wouldn't be if I wasn't a singer, I can bet you that."

When he was given *People en Espanol*'s Sexiest Man in the World title in 1998, Enrique scoffed at the dubious honor. He was so abashed by the implication that he joked with a nosy journalist, telling her that his music label had bought the cover especially for him. One thing led to another, and the next thing Enrique knew, a wire service had picked up the quote, making it look as if he'd been serious. The public was in an outrage, and demanded that the magazine print an explanation. Of course, there was nothing to explain and no conspiracy to uncover once Enrique set the record straight.

When probed about the incident, Enrique was quick to jump on the defensive, telling a reporter that "it was completely stupid. What am I supposed to say when they ask how I feel about being the 'sexiest man alive'? That it's a great accomplishment?" Of course, he was right. After all, good-looking guys are a dime a dozen, but true artists are one in a million.

One of the most positive things ever to happen to Enrique was learning how to cope with his own fame. As a young boy, he often blamed his father for not being there to take care of him or help him with his homework. He knew what fame looked and felt like, but he was unable to fully appreciate the pressure and intensity of being a world-famous singer. Now that he had his own frame of reference, Enrique was coming into a deeper understanding of his father. And although the two strong-willed men rarely agreed on anything, their bond had strengthened over the years.

At long last, Enrique understood the draw of the live audience, the feeling of being in front of millions of people and knowing that each and every one of them is happy because of his music. The intensity of those moments could not be overestimated. Like his father, who'd been pulled to the crowd like a sailor to a siren song, Enrique finally realized that performing was not just a passion, but an addiction. "I've said it many times. I wouldn't recommend this life to anyone," he elaborated. "What I would recommend is the music and the audience. The warmth you get from the audience during a concert is so good that you feel such happiness that it turns into a drug that you don't want to end, and I won't change it for anything."

EIGHT

The Language of Love

Saying good-bye to the stage would prove harder than Enrique could have ever imagined. Interacting with his fans and letting the roar of the crowd wash over him like warm waves of pure love was his reason for being. Not a moment went by that he wasn't monumentally grateful for having the chance to spread joy through his music.

The only thing that could have come between him and his fans was the studio. For much as his admirers wanted to see him on stage, they also wanted him to continue making new music. His legions of loyal followers would wait anxiously for the release of each album, trusting that Enrique would not disappoint them.

In order to keep feeding the public's wild frenzy for everything Enrique, he would have to retire to a recording studio to begin work on his third album, titled *Cosas del Amor* (The Things of Love).

Enrique's preoccupation with the subject of love

led him to craft an album that would pay homage to one of the most powerful emotions available to the human race. But it wasn't just the notion of romantic love that inspired Enrique. The love he felt for his fans, society, his family, and his music was just as crucial as the happily-ever-after variety.

At this stage of his career, when he found himself and his talent idolized by millions, Enrique could not help but feel that the world was a miraculous place, where anyone could realize their dreams no matter how far-fetched. The artist's optimism had no bounds, and *Cosas del Amor* would be an expression of this overriding gratitude for all of life's precious moments. "Some people have said how can a guy of twenty-two write such songs, but I think when you fall in love the most and when you're the most magical and most crazy is when you're young—not sixty," Enrique asserted to the *Calgary Sun*. "When you're sixty that's when you write about Medicare."

Even more intimate and passionate than his first two efforts, *Cosas del Amor* would be the culmination of his career. Enrique wanted this album to reflect his maturity, newfound wisdom, and musical acumen. Of course, he would never completely stray from his previous formula for success.

In an attempt to test the bounds of his imagination, Enrique decided to write six original songs for the album. Although he had contributed to his previous recordings, the majority of his entries were from his bygone teenage years. The twenty-three-year-old in him had at last hit upon new experiences to document and fresh sensations to share. While his childhood had been a rich soil for the first sprouts of his creativity, maturity had also sprung its own buds of musical greatness. "I wrote most of my songs when I was sixteen or seventeen," explained Enrique, "so it is only natural that people now will find an artist who is different in terms of the words, the music, and the interpretation."

Six brand-new songs, however, would not be enough to fill out an album. To finish the oeuvre, Enrique brought on songwriter/producer Rafael Perez Botija, who had also been a vital collaborator on *Vivir*. One of his first contributions to the album was "*Esperanza*," written with Chein Garcia. The meditation on love needed only the simplest of arrangements to reinforce the subdued, but resonant sound of Enrique's melodious voice.

Other notable entries included "*Dicen Por Ahi*" (They Say), a song cowritten by his old friend and mentor from Miami, Mario Martinelli. Writing a song can be a laborious process, but with his old cohort at his side, Enrique was able to complete this song in one afternoon.

Making the album had been a true labor of love. Yet, when all the final pieces were at last in place, Enrique found that he had created a masterpiece that would span all generations and cultures. Never has the language of love been as universal as in *Cosas del Amor*. "It's the kind of music you can put on with your wife or girlfriend in the car, or a romantic dinner," he informed CNN. "I tell ya, they'll just want to love you more."

His record label was duly impressed by the machinations going on in the studio. Keeping a close eye on all the proceedings, Fonovisa execs expected greatness, but could never have envisioned the utter genius of the final result.

Showing their true appreciation and feeling for their best-selling artist, the label wrote the following press material to commemorate the album's release:

> "The different songs in *Cosas del Amor* are joined by a common thread of romanticism, or better yet, knotted together by the innermost cords of a simple and intense man who has honestly devoted himself to imprinting his music with what he feels under his skin and who surrenders it without pretension, without ruse, for others to interpret, analyze, and dream inspired by that eternal emotion called love."

When the album hit the record store shelves on September 22, 1998, speculation about Enrique's love life soared to an all-time high. Anxious to break a story about the singer's secret love affairs, journalists encouraged Enrique to divulge the inspiration for *Cosas del Amor*. Surely, this album must have been written for the love of Enrique's life.

"Who's the lucky girl?" they asked.

"Come on, Enrique. The people want to know," they goaded.

Trying to explain that the album was not dedicated to one girl so much as to a whole way of life was impossible. Nor could Enrique convey that writing love songs was merely a way of getting over some of the heartache from his past. So while most reporters continued to believe that the album was a celebration of a special someone, the truth of the matter was that Enrique's songs were actually a therapeutic outlet for the sorrow of lost love. "Every time I write—I mean, I write about what's going on in my life," he reported to *Good Morning America*. "So there's got to be something—I mean, I've got to get dumped to write a good song."

As the ultimate romantic hero for Spanish-speaking audiences worldwide, Enrique was in for some more surprises. Not only would the media try to pair him off in real-life liaisons, but he was soon being courted to star in a Latin soap opera. Seeing that Enrique had the grace, style, and charm of a leading man, soap opera producer Juan Osorio began soliciting Enrique's services for his new daytime drama.

When he first received the call, Enrique was flattered. Acting had always interested him, but he had never thought about pursuing it as a career. The media had also jumped on this latest development, reporting that the young singer was seriously considering the offer. But no matter how tempting the proposition was, Enrique was forced to turn it down. Not only did he not feel confident about his acting skills, but he did not want to be distracted from his music. "No, I cannot do it," Enrique explained. "Osorio is convincing me to try, but my commitment, my passion is the music. I am a terrible actor."

Up until now, the careers of Enrique and his father had run on parallel tracks. But when the offer to act came in, Enrique strayed from the path Julio had taken. Having made a couple of unsuccessful films, Julio was always complaining about his poor acting skills and the bad choices he'd made when it came to movies. In an attempt to learn from his father's example, Enrique spared himself and the audience the agony of having to sit through his own attempts at acting.

Disappointed by his response, Osorio began petitioning for the next best thing—Enrique's music for his soundtrack. If he couldn't have Enrique, then he would gladly have his music. This was an offer that the young singer could not refuse. Having already rejected Osorio once, Enrique felt compelled to assist the producer, and offered him a few songs from which to choose.

But if Enrique thought that contributing a few songs to a soap opera would put an end to his image as the ultimate heartthrob, he was sorely mistaken. His next opportunity to woo millions of women came in the form of invitations to judge and sing at several beauty pageants. Who else but the Sexiest Man in the World could be asked to select the sexiest woman alive? It was a perfect cross-marketing opportunity, and made for a lot of sensational headlines.

Enrique's first beauty pageant came in 1998 when he was asked to judge the finalists and perform at the Miss Venezuela pageant. Unwilling to lose out on the chance to be surrounded by a hundred beautiful women, Enrique promptly agreed to the offer.

This connection to the world of beauty pageants became even more pronounced when Enrique was rumored to be dating former Miss Universe Alicia Machado. The magazine *Hola!* was the first to break the story. One source at the magazine reported that the pair was spotted dining in a restaurant and holding hands at the beach. The publication also reported that the rumors were substantiated by photographs of the couple taking long walks along the beach.

"Those rumors have been confirmed with photographs of the pair in a paradise-like beach of Miami having a romantic and calm stroll," reported the magazine. "The friendship that doubtlessly exists between Enrique and Alicia could be becoming something more serious."

Although this was not the first time that the press attempted to link Enrique with a Latina celebrity, including Paty Manterola and the Spanish model Estefanía Luyk, none of his earlier romances had been surrounded by so much controversy. As Miss Universe, Alicia Machado accepted her title weighing only 118 pounds. Through the duration of her reign, however, Alicia gained some weight. The Venezuelan beauty was said to have gained fifty pounds during her reign. Of course, that would never do for the winner of the Miss Universe pageant. Some sources reported that she was being pressured to step down from her post, but owner and CEO of the Miss Universe pageant, Donald Trump, insisted that she would not have to give up her title, but should consider trying to lose the weight.

These revelations made for some sensational tabloid fodder, especially when Alicia announced that she was proud of the way she looked and wanted to find a man who would love her for her curvy figure. She explained that she would never settle for anything less than "a man who loves the real Alicia Machado, the woman who I am, thin or fat, famous or not." And when talk of Enrique's involvement began to brew, the press had simply assumed that Alicia had found the guy she had been searching for.

Whether or not the two were actually involved in a relationship, one thing was for certain: keeping it under wraps would prove more difficult than either of them could have anticipated. Newspapers were anxious to get photos of the beautiful young couple, and when those failed to surface, the speculation of the press seemed only to increase. "Enrique and Alicia are young," a journalist at *Hola!* reported. "Both are free to fall in love and there is someone who is sure that the miracle has already taken place. Everything indicates that the pair wishes to maintain its relationship with discretion."

For all their talk of secrecy and discretion, the press didn't miss a single opportunity to question Enrique about his alleged love affair. During one press conference at the Miss Venezuela pageant held in Caracas, Enrique began a press conference only to find himself being grilled on his love life and Alicia's place within it. What made the story even more fascinating was that Alicia was scheduled to attend the pageant that evening. Even though they were not seen together in public, the grapevine was abuzz during the entire competition.

In an attempt to keep the gossipmongers at bay, Enrique admitted to being nothing more than friends with the beauty queen. "Alicia is charming, I have known her for two years. And the truth is that I arrived very late at Caracas and I did not have time to speak with her, but I am going to."

Having said that, Enrique found himself on the receiving end of even more attention from the tabloid press. Colombian model and pinup Sofia Vergara was just one of the many women who was alleged to have had an affair with Enrique (she was also linked to both Luis Miguel and Ricky Martin). While Sofia made a pointed effort to dispel the mushroom cloud of gossip, saying "Enrique and I [are] only friends, although I am enamored with his last disc," the talk raged on.

Enrique was also adamant about refuting the accusations. He had met Sofia through his sister, and their relationship had always been strictly platonic. That was his story and he would stick to it.

Trying to be as candid as possible without revealing too much about their private lives is a struggle that every celebrity must face. But for someone like Enrique, who prides himself on his honesty, not telling the whole truth can seem as if he's doing a disservice to his fans.

Of course, even Enrique had to admit that something as serious as a person's love life should be kept under wraps. Giving himself over to his fans via his music was one thing, but it was important to draw the line. As things stood, Enrique was a most generous celebrity. Few superstars spent as much time getting to know their fans. But when it came down to protecting the people he cared about, the young singer was all about security and discretion.

Having seen the ill effects that living in the public eye had had on his father, Enrique was determined not to make the same mistakes. Too many of his father's romances were broken off due to his highly publicized affairs. And although Enrique wasn't planning on getting involved in more than one romance at a time, he didn't want idle gossip compromising his relationships. "I keep my private life private," said Enrique, "and if I had one or have one, no one will know."

Although the demand for information on Enrique's love life was always high, he never let on to the fact that he was in a relationship. Of course, as a normal red-blooded young man, he craved the companionship of women. He needed the kind of emotional intimacy that he never had growing up. Finding the right woman, however, would prove to be very difficult. Although he had several meaningful relationships in the past, he was unable to find the love that he was looking for. "I wasn't a major reject, but I was rejected enough to get hurt a bunch of times," he admitted to *USA Today*. "That's OK. There's someone for everyone. Wait—it'll happen."

His extensive touring and publicity appearances only served to exacerbate the difficulty of meeting that special someone. Being on the road and traveling around the world didn't leave much time for romance, nor was this itinerary conducive to sustaining a relationship. Still, whenever he had the chance, Enrique always made sure to pencil in some time for dating.

Despite his busy workaday life, the young singer claims that his top priority is falling in love and having a family. And although he would never abandon his music career, he would slow down considerably for the right woman. "If I fall in love with a woman, I would love to marry her and have many children with her."

Some say that finding someone to love is the easy part; being ready for love is what's really difficult. Whether Enrique was mature enough or emotionally prepared for a committed relationship remained to be seen. He was, after all, still in his early twenties. And no matter how much he tried to keep his feet on the ground, it was hard for him to resist the millions of attractive women who flocked to his stage, his doorstep, and even his dressing room.

Another factor that prevented the young man from falling in love was an inability to be as intimate with his girlfriends as he was with his fans. Onstage, he was the perfect man—confident, strong, and secure. In the real world, however, Enrique was filled with self-doubt and insecurities. Much as he tried to reveal himself to his girlfriends, Enrique was unable to take the emotional risks that long-term relationships required. The rejection he experienced as a young boy left lasting scars that would take years to heal. "I'm more romantic in my music than in real life," he told the *Washington Post*. "I say stuff in my music that I would never dare say face-to-face; I'd be too embarrassed."

Still, Enrique was a romantic at heart. Not a moment went by that he didn't think about his future bride. Having a blissful family oasis of his own creation had always been his dream. And now that he was old enough to have anything he wanted, Enrique couldn't help but ruminate on the joys of one day becoming a family man. No matter how uncertain his love life was, he could take comfort in knowing that if love should ever find him, he would be able to recognize it for what it was. "You notice when someone really loves you, I mean just by the way they kiss you, just by the way they look at you, just by the way they treat you," he explained to the *Washington Post*. "You know, you might not notice the first day or the second day, but after a while you do notice."

Enrique obviously knew a good thing when he saw it, and that translated into finding the right woman as well. Just any girl with a pretty face would not do for the soulful and mentally agile young man. He needed someone who could bring something to the relationship. Whether it was a passion for her career, talent, or wisdom, the woman who hoped to capture the young singer's heart would have her work cut out for her. "Me, I just want to have one girlfriend," he expressed to *People.* "I've met so many beautiful girls with no brains. But there hasn't been that special one that has clicked. It's so lonely sometimes."

When it came to women, Enrique was one man who knew what he wanted. Rather than trying to date girls who were all flash and no substance, he sought out those women with whom he could form long-lasting friendships. And for a man who could date anyone in the world, that was a rarity in itself.

Asking Enrique about the kind of women he preferred to date had become second nature for those reporters lucky enough to get close to him. But instead of hearing the stock response of "a good-looking girl with a nice personality," the media was treated to a candid and frank discussion of his likes and dislikes. "You know what turns me on in a girl? Talent," he confided in *Rolling Stone.* "You meet a girl who's maybe not so beautiful physically, but she's a great singer or dancer. And that, for me, is the biggest turn-on."

Judging by his predilection for serious and intelligent actresses like Juliette Lewis (*Cape Fear, Natural Born Killers*), it is clear that Enrique is one guy who likes to be challenged. "I think she's a good actress, and she's very sexy," he asserted. "I especially liked her in *What's Eating Gilbert Grape?* I don't know what it is; maybe because she's talented—there's just something about her."

Talented or not, every girl deserves to feel special, and Enrique is just the man for the job. Whether it's his fans or a longtime steady, the women in Enrique's life rarely find cause for complaint. And when you consider the fact that he is always singing about being abandoned or rejected, it is clear that the need to please is rooted as much in his childhood as it is in his cultural background. "I grew up with very Latin manners, whether it was opening doors or at the dinner table or the way you act when you talk to someone or meet someone," explained Enrique. "It's a very respectful way."

While love continued to elude Enrique, his relationship with his family had evolved through the years. Because he was busy touring the world and cutting multiplatinum albums, Enrique didn't have as much time for family visits as he would have liked. He was so frazzled by his hectic schedule, that he even had to make appointments for his phone calls to Isabel. While their relationship was as close as ever, the majority of their mother-son bonding sessions occurred over the phone, just as they had during Enrique's youth. "Only when I go to Spain do I get to see my mother," he explained, "and then it is somewhat difficult due to my schedule. I miss them all very much."

He and his older brother Julio Jr., however, had grown much tighter with the march of time. In 1998, Julio Jr. shocked the family by announcing that he, too, wanted to begin a recording career. Of course, his path would in no way resemble Enrique's. Not only had he come right out with his intentions to make music, but his first album would be sung entirely in English. "If he has talent, then he will do fine," observed Enrique. "But it will have nothing to do with his name being Julio Iglesias. I didn't even know that he liked music."

Although Julio Jr. had shown an interest in show business during college, acting in an NBC series, *Out of the Blue*, and modeling for Versace and Gap, singing had never crossed his mind. But seeing how successful his younger brother and father were, the concept of joining them wasn't entirely far-fetched. For a while there it seemed that if you were born an Iglesias, you were destined to sing or perish. "I have another kid now who is going to have an album," Julio proudly reported to the *Chicago Sun-Times*. "So I am going to have a family of singers, like the Von Trapp family."

Enrique's sister Chabeli was the only one who wasn't involved with music. But show business was another matter altogether. Ever since she started modeling at the age of fourteen, Chabeli had enjoyed a life in the spotlight. Most recently, she has signed on to host her own talk show on the US Spanish network Univision. Although she had worked in television since she was eighteen years old, this would mark her first voyage into the fertile commercial grounds of the United States.

Soon after securing her own talk show, Chabeli went on to marry twenty-eight-year-old Ricardo Bofill Jr., who worked as a scriptwriter for the European television channel Canal Plus. Enrique's sister was thrilled about the prospect of starting her own family. But before she could make the dream a reality, the couple announced that they would be separating.

And if that wasn't bad enough, Chabeli had a terrible car accident in 1999. When the news broke that Chabeli had been thrown from her car after it collided with an oncoming vehicle, the family rushed to the Los Angeles Medical Center where she was being treated for minor fractures and bruises. Julio, who recalled his own car accident all too vividly, was also on hand to take care of his only daughter. Fortunately for the family, Chabeli recovered in a matter of weeks.

Tragedy has a way of bringing people together, and that was the case for Julio and Enrique. Although they had buried the hatchet long ago, there were still some competitive instincts that gave spark to their relationship. No matter how often father and son denied allegations of friendly competition, the little things they said throughout their careers told a different story.

On one occasion, Julio came forward with the opinion that his children had profited from having him for a father. And even if the comment was a lapse in judgment, it revealed more than he'd ever intended. "They are lucky to be my children," Julio told the *South China Morning Post*. "They have great luck in that doors have opened for them so rapidly."

Although Julio thought that he was telling it like it was when a journalist from the *Chicago Sun-Times* asked about the ongoing comparisons and charges of nepotism, the gloves came off and Enrique spoke his mind. "It's pathetic. Even after I won the Grammy, I heard this girl say, 'Oh, you won a Grammy because your dad is Julio Iglesias,' and you know the funny thing is that last year my dad was nominated for a Grammy and he didn't win. I don't like to get into it but I'm tired of hearing, 'Do you think you sell more records because of your dad?' Well, right now in the US, I sell more records than my father. So it would seem a little contradictory that people are buying the records only for who my dad is."

While Enrique might not have been staying up late to tabulate his father's record sales, he was well aware of who was outselling whom. Now that he was doing so well, he could not resist tooting his own horn. "Please do not introduce me as the son of Julio Iglesias," said Enrique. "I'm very proud of my father, but when you read *Billboard* now, you see Enrique Iglesias."

While it may seem that both father and son had some issues to work out, it was clear that their problems began long before Enrique had even considered singing. A year after his first album's release, Julio claimed that he had not heard Enrique sing. "I have still not heard him sing, but they tell me that he is wonderful," he said.

Julio was undoubtedly saddened by his son's detachment. When Julio Jr. first announced his plans to record an album, his father was the first person he told. Julio and his namesake had never experienced any tension, and he wished that Enrique would have been more open about his career.

Whether the competition between the two Iglesiases began when Enrique struck out on his own was uncertain. In their attempt to pit father and son against one another, the media could have had a much greater impact on putting the two singers at odds. Then again, the music business itself might have been the culprit. The industry's competitive nature ensured that everyone knew their rightful place within the hierarchy.

Back in June 1997, Enrique and Julio had unknowingly gotten themselves into a tense situation when both were booked to give concerts in Chicago. While Enrique sold out the entire 18,000-seat Rosemont Horizon, his father was scheduled to perform at the 4,500-seat Rosemont Theatre. Although they never discussed the disparity of their venues, father and son were undoubtedly conscious of what had transpired.

Seeing Enrique's star rise while his own had hit a plateau, Julio was even more determined to reclaim his title as the highest-selling artist in the world. Resentment, however, was not what spurred on his increased efforts. It was the spirit of good, old-fashioned rivalry that Julio could never resist. "The first thing for him is his job. Even though he takes care of his children, he is also very competitive," explained *Exito* magazine's entertainment editor, Itziar Bilbao. "He says for him, Enrique's success is like a motivation for him, something that makes him run faster."

Another incident that threatened the familial ties occurred when both Enrique and Julio were nominated for the same award at the American Music Awards. This time, however, Julio would arise victorious, walking away with the Best Latin Artist trophy. While Enrique was happy for his father, he was determined to keep a sense of perspective in all things concerning his family. "Actually, it doesn't happen that much," he told the *Buffalo News*. "But when it does, I just look at him just like another singer."

The award show was just one example of the

mental distinctions that Enrique needed to make between Julio the singer and Julio the father. Confusing one for the other could have disastrous consequences for his family life. For all their disagreements, Enrique cared more for his family than for anything else in the world. "I get along perfectly with my father and with all my family. I just don't see them a lot," Enrique stated to *Florida Today*. "I'm always working and he's always working. To tell you the truth, I separate myself as much as possible in my career, so that's where all this talk of conflict comes from."

Enrique's assertion was an astute one. While the media would have picked up on the father/son parallel on their own, they might not have covered the alleged friction with such fervent zeal had Enrique been more open to his father's counsel. Unwilling to shirk responsibility, Enrique took full credit for the controversy that his decision to be independent had inspired. Feeling somewhat guilty for having unwittingly incited so much malicious gossip, Enrique went out of his way to refute the rumors of a bitter family feud. The vehemence with which he did so is evidenced by the following retort to a "feuding Iglesiases" question: "I never said that! I don't know where they got that from," a visibly frustrated Enrique told one newspaper. "It would be stupid of me to say that. I never said that at all."

The singer would not allow idle gossip to get in the way of his love for his father. Professional and temperamental differences aside, Enrique and Julio had a strong bond that was based on mutual interests and family. While Enrique could readily list his father's flaws when probed, his love for him allowed him to overlook the minor things, and vice versa.

The news that Julio's companion of eight years, Miranda Rinsburger, was with child brought Enrique nothing but happiness. He wanted only the best for his father, and expressed this sentiment clearly by publicly congratulating Julio on the impending birth. "It's cool," he responded to the *Chicago Sun-Times*. "I'm happy for my dad."

Whatever drama the media might have tried to orchestrate, Enrique and Julio were making it abundantly clear that they would not fall prey to any more underhanded stratagems. By 1998, most of the reports of the Iglesias battle had subsided. The press had finally learned that trying to stir up trouble between the Iglesiases was the fastest way to get an interview cancelled. Lately, the only comments that Enrique makes about his father are overwhelmingly positive, leading the casual observer to believe that any differences that the two might have had in the past are now laid to rest. "He is my father," Enrique explained to Diane Sawyer. "I'm one of his biggest fans not only as a singer, but as a father."

As much as he might have once loathed to admit it, Enrique had to acknowledge the fact that his father had broken down many barriers in the music industry and in his own life. By providing an example of unlimited potential and opportunity, Julio allowed Enrique the luxury of dreaming the impossible dream. Enrique had music coursing through his veins, and watching his father make a living as a singer had undoubtedly inspired his first foray into song.

Like the rest of the Spanish music community, who had watched Julio reach one unattainable goal after another, Enrique could not help feeling indebted to his father for spreading Latin music throughout the world. As the universal performer, Julio appealed to people from all walks of life. His uncommon talent and awe-inspiring charisma had paved the way for numerous Latin singers, including Enrique.

"A lot of people think me and my father don't get along," Enrique expressed to the *Washington Post*. "Of course we get along, and when it comes down to the real stuff, I'd kill for my father. I'm his number one fan. What my father has accomplished no one will ever accomplish. What I'm trying to accomplish now with Spanish music, he made easier and accomplished it twenty years ago and that's amazing."

Julio had also grown much more calm and content with the years. While Enrique's secretive behavior in the early stages of his career had caused him some pain, time had soothed his disappointment. Today, Julio understands why Enrique had to do everything on his own. Had he been in his son's position, he probably would have done the same thing. The happy equilibrium that finally prevailed within their relationship was a source of tremendous pleasure for Julio. And now that his feelings of paternal love were again at an all-time high, Julio could finally express what he had been thinking all along. "I think it's amazing," Julio said of Enrique's success. "He is an amazing kid. He has a lot of class, a lot of charm, a lot of talent. He is young, he is nice looking. He has everything. Sometimes I look at him and I don't believe this guy is so young and so successful. I adore him," he said during a recent tour stop in Las Vegas.

To be completely honest, it took Enrique many years to get over the disappointments and frustrations he'd had to deal with as a boy. Although he had once thought that he would never get over his father's hands-off parenting style, at twenty-seven years of age, Enrique could honestly say that the times he'd spent alone in the house, waiting for Julio to come along and tell him that everything was going to be all right, were finally forgotten.

As he matured, Enrique came to discover that the very thing he'd blamed his father for, namely leaving him to fend for himself, was the thing that had allowed him to become such a success. If it hadn't been for the self-reliance he'd gained at an early age, Enrique might never have had the courage to begin writing music. And if he hadn't been left alone, he wouldn't have had the chance to use his solitude for writing. More importantly, had he never developed into a worldwide sensation, he never would have gained the sharp insight into his father's true character. All things considered, Enrique's and Julio's relationship has now come full circle.

What had begun as a rocky road for the Iglesias family turned into a successful quest for the holy grail of contentment. Enrique finally accepted his father, his mother was happy living with her husband in Spain, and his siblings were also leading healthy and prosperous lives.

The charmed quality of the family's saga was not lost on Julio either. According to him, life didn't get any better than his. "I am happy, and it is not for nothing. I am about to have a son; my son Enrique is a marvel; my son Julio has a wonderful voice and sings very well, so I'm going to have two star children; Chabeli is really fine; my parents are alive; and I continue singing. I cannot ask more to life. In twenty years, the only one thing that will keep me happy will be the success of my children. One of the greatest joys of my life is seeing what is happening to them."

NINE

Wild, Wild Enrique!

His first tour, in support of *Vivir*, had seen Enrique travel to thirteen countries and perform before some 720,000 spectators. This flawless track record left no doubt that Enrique was indeed a world-class entertainer. Using the momentum of his past success as a springboard, Enrique decided to follow up the release of *Cosas del Amor* with a tour that would eclipse his last by spanning the entire globe.

His prospects were truly unlimited, especially when Enrique found out that McDonald's had offered to sponsor the US leg of his tour. Luring such a heavyweight sponsor into his corner was a major accomplishment, usually reserved only for the biggest names in the business. Enrique had originally crossed paths with the sponsor while volunteering on behalf of the Ronald McDonald House Charities. He had always shown a great interest in helping young children, and was especially committed to the cause that raised money for AIDS research and educational opportunities. "I help the Ronald McDonald's fund," he explained. "That is how McDonald's became involved in sponsoring my '99 tour. Besides, I love hamburgers."

Scheduled to kick off in New York's Madison Square Garden on January 16, 1999, the *Cosas del Amor* tour would take Enrique through thirty-three cities around the country. And now that McDonald's was on board, Enrique was even more confident about the ensuing tour. "Having grown up with McDonald's, I'm delighted to be collaborating with them on this exciting project," he explained. "With the help of the Golden Arches, I can bring my music to millions of people across the country."

The success of the tour was made all the more important by the fact that a portion of Enrique's concert proceeds would benefit RMHC/HACER scholarship program (Hispanic American Commitment to Education Resources). The singer wanted to do as much for his chosen cause as possible. He had already taped several public service announcements for the organization, but the tour would allow him to make an ever bigger contribution. "McDonald's is honored to be associated with Enrique Iglesias and to be able to bring this great talent to our customers across the country," said Marta Gerdes, McDonald's director of US marketing. "This tour provides an excellent opportunity, not only to raise funds for the RMHC/HACER scholarship program, but also to increase the awareness of HACER with Enrique's support. This tour is our way of saying 'thank you' to not only our most loyal Hispanic customers but to the 25 million consumers that visit our restaurants every day throughout the US."

In order to promote his tour, Enrique was also asked to make his acting debut in a McDonald's commercial. The thirty-second Spanish-language spot was aired repeatedly during the summer to ensure the highest possible attendance.

Although the trip was promoted with a "Coming to America" theme, Enrique's two platinum albums showed that he already had an extremely avid following in the States. In fact, Spanish-speaking fans from the US comprised a large portion of Enrique's fan base. Having grown up in Miami, he was, for all intents and purposes, an American, by no means unfamiliar with the country or its language. Still, some reporters loved to play up the Latin-singer-makes-good-in-the-US concept, writing that Enrique's success in America was a recent phenomenon.

But Enrique didn't let these reports confound the issue. Even if he had lost sight of the fact that he was adored in the United States, his American fans would never let him forget just how much they loved him. Enrique was extremely grateful for the warm reception he received at each and every stop. He could not have predicted the kind of commotion that his presence incited. "It feels great," he told CNN. "When you're out there, your audience is responding, amazing, and you're on US soil. It just tells you that Latino music in the US is growing so strong."

Enrique understood what some marketers could not, and that was that America was one of the most fecund breeding grounds for Latin music. As one of the country's fastest-growing demographics, Latino

Americans had always supported talented artists of Latin origin. "I have a great audience," he conveyed to MTV. "You know, there's a great Latino audience in the US. It's funny, because a lot of people say, 'So how's it in South America?' 'How's it in Spain?' What these people don't realize is that the biggest Spanish market is in the US. I mean, there's 30 million Spanish-speaking people in the US that love their music, that love their singers, and actually, when you have a hit in the Spanish market . . . I hate saying 'market' too . . . but it doesn't only hit the girls, or should I say, the young girls. It hits everywhere, whether you're forty, fifty, sixty, whether you're fifteen, whether you're a boy, whether you're a girl."

Having roots in both the Latin and American cultures, Enrique was always torn between the desire to sing in English and in Spanish. Growing up, most of his musical influences had been English. Indeed, the first song he had ever written had been entirely in English. "I grew up in Miami since I was seven years old, so I grew up listening to a lot of Anglo music. I had huge idols like Billy Joel, Bruce Springsteen, Tom Petty, and I started writing in English and singing in English. Then I stopped that and I went into Spanish, and it started going well in Spanish, so I was just waiting for the right time to do it in English."

Unlike his brother, Julio Jr., Enrique had decided to sing in Spanish. It was a calculated decision, but not one that could change overnight. Because he had become so accustomed to writing in Spanish, Enrique found that most of his songs could not be smoothly translated into English. It was just too difficult to find the right material that would sound good in either language. "On this album I have a song that was sung in the '80s called 'Only You' and that melody was so simple that when I put Spanish lyrics to it, it sounded good," he told the *Chicago Sun-Times*. "But I think it's very seldom that you find songs like that, that just works well both ways. If I sang my Spanish songs in English they would sound real corny and vice versa. But I will sing in English someday. I just have to find the right song and my style."

While Enrique had first thought that the US tour was his sole purpose for trekking through the country, it turned out to be a mere prelude of bigger things to come. Unbeknownst to Enrique, movie star and recording artist extraordinaire Will Smith had stopped in to check out one of his electrifying showcases. Blown away by the power of Enrique's stage presence and magnificent voice, Smith stopped by after the show to congratulate the singer. Enrique was extremely flattered by Smith's approbation, but didn't give the incident much thought until he received a call from Smith asking him to contribute a song to the soundtrack of his new movie, *Wild Wild West*.

As a huge fan of Smith's, Enrique was overwhelmed by the offer. He had seen all of Smith's movies, and savored the opportunity to work together. "I'm a big Will Smith fan," Enrique recounted the incident to the New York *Daily News*. "So when he called me, I was like 'Whoa, Will Smith!' I was really excited."

Now came the hard part. Although Enrique was never big on giving his songs to movie soundtracks, he had heard enough about the movie to know that he wanted to get a piece of the action. So in order to confirm the agreement, Enrique searched through his songs to find an English song that would knock Smith's socks off. After a few moments' thought, he knew just what song to pick. *"Bailamos"* had been written several months prior to his tour, and had been languishing in his directory of songs ever since. Now was the perfect opportunity to bring this beautiful and passionate ode to dance out of the storage bin.

The movie producers were floored by Enrique's submission. First of all, they had not expected such a speedy reply. Secondly, they couldn't believe that Enrique had kept the track under wraps for as long as he had. It was that good. "To tell you the truth, I've never been a big fan of soundtracks," Enrique revealed to *All Star News.* "There are sometimes songs on them that go to waste. They are never singles, but when I sent [the producers] this song, they said they wanted to make it a single. That made me feel a lot better. I fell in love with the song five months ago and I didn't want it to go to waste. I had a lot of faith in it."

While recording the single, Enrique didn't want to take any chances. The opportunity to participate in this soundtrack was too important to his career. Realizing that this blockbuster feature film could lead to an English record deal, Enrique was determined to make his song stand out among the other featured tracks. "When I'm making a record, I will take home two or three, maybe five, versions and listen to all of them over and over until I know which one I want," he conveyed to the *Daily News.* "I'm not looking for the one where all the music is perfect. I'm looking for the one that has the right feeling. The one that moves me."

Enrique had planned to record in English for as long as he could remember, but he thought it would be years before he would ever get that chance. As with most good news, the invitation to contribute to *Wild Wild West* had come completely out of the blue. "I never thought it was going to come so soon," he told MTV. "I don't know, it's come to me pretty natural. A lot of my influence was very Anglo growing up, so it's good to finally be able to work in English and actually put a lot of my influences in my songs that I am recording."

To really package himself for his English-language debut, Enrique would need to pull out all the stops, including making a video, or two, to accompany his new single. Shot at the Universal lot, the first video featured him as the gun-slinging lone rider, dancing in a courtyard with a bevy of seductive señoritas. A second video was also shot to reflect the song's more contemporary side. That follow-up features Enrique singing at a lively nightclub, while sneaking in some amorous moments with an otherwise engaged young woman.

"*Bailamos*" was to be released a couple of weeks after Will Smith's "Wild Wild West" single. Enrique didn't know what to expect. Ricky Martin's success boded well for his own future, but then again, Enrique knew that one never could predict the public's reaction. The singer was finally put out of his misery when his single hit the stores and the airwaves. There was no denying that Enrique had scored his first English-language hit.

From its first day on the radio, "*Bailamos*" had established itself as one of the most requested tracks in Miami and Los Angeles. Soon, the whole country was in the throes of Enrique fever. "The Latin influence is where it's at today in pop music," Tom Poleman, program director of Z–100, told the *Daily News*. "We're seeing the kind of influx of Latin stars that we saw with country stars last year. Ordinarily at Z–100, we're pretty conservative about adding records by artists we haven't played before, but when we heard '*Bailamos*' we went on it right away. Our listeners love it."

While Enrique was making his own impact on the music scene, the year of 1999 would see many other talented Latin singers coming out of the woodwork. After Ricky Martin had swept the nation with his rousing single, "Livin' la Vida Loca," Brooklyn-born Jennifer Lopez was heating things up with her soulful album *On the 6*, and other Latin favorites like Marc Anthony, Luis Miguel, and Chris Perez were waiting in the wings. For a while there, it seemed that the whole country had gone loco over Latin music.

The success of Latin music, however, was no overnight sensation. It had always been very popular among the Latino community. The genre's low profile could only be attributed to radio stations' and marketers' shared penchant for ignoring the Spanish-speaking audience. When artists like Ricky Martin, Jennifer Lopez, and Enrique Iglesias came on the scene, most Americans were getting their first taste of Latin music, while the Latinos were hearing the same sounds they had been listening to all along. "It's a different world now," Jeff Ayeroff, co-president of the Sony's Work Group label, told *Rolling Stone*. "It doesn't take much logic to see that the larger urban centers have huge Spanish-speaking populations. Look at Los Angeles: The biggest stations are all Latin stations. New York has it, Florida has it; Texas, Arizona, Chicago—the American continent is a Latin continent. I don't think it's any great genius move—we're all very clever lemmings in this business."

While radio stations were playing the maracas out of Enrique, Ricky Martin, and Jennifer Lopez, MTV had also embraced the Latin explosion by playing the artists' videos back-to-back and even running a full-hour documentary on the Latin music phenomenon. Tom Calderone, senior vice president of MTV, explained, "our audience doesn't look at music like other generations have. They don't put it in boxes like 'Latin' or 'rap' or 'alternative.' They base it on the individual's personality as well as on the music."

Whether it was the sex appeal, the dynamic personalities, or the impassioned music of the crossover pop stars, mainstream audiences found the new crop of Latino artists simply irresistible. "I think Americans are discovering Latinos," Enrique opined. "Also, Latinos are a very romantic people, and there's a sexiness to [the music]. There's a nice beat, a nice popping sound."

But it wasn't only the people who were seduced by Enrique's unique brand of Latin pop. Critics were also bowled over by the heartfelt and seductive single. One music reviewer for *Florida Today* had this to say: "The Grammy winner's first English-language offering has all the makings of a smash, with or without the burgeoning Latin-pop explosion. Sporting a flamenco guitar and other Southwestern influences amid a contemporary shuffling beat, '*Bailamos*' moves along at a pace that's much more relaxed than

Martin's 'Livin' la Vida Loca,' but it still is lively enough to work up a bit of a froth on the dance floor circuit, especially after it gets a tasty remix treatment, which is bound to be in the works."

Another critic for *University Wire* selected "*Bailamos*" as the best song to come off the *Wild Wild West* soundtrack, writing, "There is also plenty of fluff from relatively unknown artists who Smith is trying to make stars out of. He does manage to hit the jackpot once—with Enrique Iglesias, of course, and his deserving hit '*Bailamos*.' Judging on the look of things with the current Latin pop movement, though, Iglesias probably wouldn't have needed this 'boost' from Smith to have become successful in the States. Smith was just in the right place in the right time in choosing him to appear."

The unanimous appreciation of Enrique's new single in the US led to invitations from the some of most prestigious and widely watched television shows in the country. His first mission was to sing live at the Lincoln Center Plaza for *Good Morning America*. Ricky Martin had also performed his hit single "Livin' la Vida Loca" only a month before at Rockefeller Center for *The Today Show*, and now Enrique would have his chance to stop traffic in the already-congested streets of Manhattan.

From there, Enrique was ushered to appear on the female-oriented talk show *The View*, and then to sing alongside Will Smith on a special edition of *Oprah*. With so much exposure to the US public, Enrique was put on the hot seat. Reporters who had never heard of him prior to his English single's release were acting as if he had just come on the music scene. Many had no idea that Enrique had signed his first record label contract when he was only twenty years old.

The fact that most of the English-speaking public was oblivious to his background didn't bother Enrique as much as one would have thought. He knew that he was in it for the long haul. In fact, there was not a doubt in his mind that he would be making music long after "*Bailamos*" had become just another foggy memory. "I've been hearing 'flavor of the month' since my first record," he expressed to the New York *Daily News*. "Well, my second record sold five million copies. My third record is selling millions. That's not flavor of the month. Music is my career."

On June 10, 1999, only a few weeks after the release of "*Bailamos*," Enrique found himself in the middle of a full-scale bidding war. Seeing that he had breakthrough potential, executives from BMG, Warner Bros., and Universal/Interscope were dying to sign Enrique to their record companies, and were throwing out all kinds of numbers in order to woo him to their side. But Enrique was not about to go with the highest bidder. Indeed, money was the least of his concerns. "I hate to talk about money," he told the *Daily News*. "If people are thinking about how much money you make, it distracts them from your music. I don't mean just fans, but also the press, the media. It's like a basketball player who signs a big contract. It seems like after that, no matter what he does, that number is always mentioned. To me, it's not about money. In fact, the new contract I will sign is not with the company that offered me the highest amount of money."

What concerned Enrique most was finding a record label that would support his commitment to making music in both Spanish and English. In order to do that, however, the label would need to have a solid understanding and admiration for Latin music, something that was very important to Enrique. "I gotta remember something—what got me here was Spanish," he told *Time* magazine. "If it wasn't for my Spanish record sales, I wouldn't have these record companies after me."

When Interscope co-chairman Jimmy Iovine came to see one of Enrique's concerts, he was convinced that Enrique was just the man he had been looking for. The performance was so powerful and the fans were so rabid, that he began negotiations almost immediately after the concert. "That night was very exciting," Iovine told *Billboard* magazine. "As deep as we're into technology, with TV and the Internet, to actually go and see a live show with that level of enthusiasm and excitement was a very moving experience. That reaction from the audience was genuine and astounding."

When it came down to the final three bidders, Enrique and manager, Fernan Martinez chose to sign with Universal/Interscope. The money was good, but it was the label's size and dedication to targeting the Latin market that finally clinched the deal. "Universal is the biggest label in the world, which can give Enrique the international exposure he needs," Martinez explained. "And Universal needed an artist like Enrique who feels at home culturally everywhere he goes, from the US to the Philippines where his mother was born."

Jimmy Iovine and the entire staff at Interscope

were ecstatic that Enrique had chosen to make their label his creative home. Iovine was certain that once Enrique's musical talents combined with the label's industry muscle, there would be no stopping his domination of music charts throughout the world. "He is an extraordinary talent and this is a wonderful opportunity for us," Iovine told *Billboard* magazine. "He already has an amazing fan base, he sings great, and he looks incredible. We consider ourselves very fortunate and look forward to a very exciting relationship."

Anxious to extract the precious product from their latest find, Interscope records encouraged Enrique to go into the studio and begin building a foundation for his first English album. With a tentative release date set for November 1999, the singer had his work cut out for him. Not only would he have to complete promoting his chart-topping single *"Bailamos"* throughout the world, but he would also have to follow through with the European segment of the *Cosas del Amor* tour. The pressure was strong enough to push a lesser artist right over the edge, but Enrique managed to stay sane by taking things one step at a time. "I'm going to go into the studio," he explained during *Good Morning America*. "Right now, it's just—this is the first English single, '*Bailamos*.' But I'm concentrated on that. And I'm going to go into the studio, I'm going to see what comes out."

He even made time for a meeting of the minds with producer Brian Rawling, who had produced Cher's hit album *Believe*. Interscope had paired the two artists in hope of creating as magical a collaboration as the one Rawling had shared with Cher. Their gut instinct proved to be right on target. No sooner had Enrique and Rawling discussed their respective visions for the album, than it became abundantly clear that Enrique's English-language debut would be all that Interscope and the public had hoped for, and more.

Auspicious beginnings aside, Enrique was beginning to tire of the whole "crossover" concept. As far as he knew, Americans had always been receptive to his music. And the fact that he would be singing in English was inconsequential in the big scheme of things. With all the hype, media coverage, and performances, all eyes turned to Enrique, and he couldn't help feeling somewhat stifled by the collective expectations.

"Everyone is talking about this whole Latino movement and this 'crossover,'" he asserted to MTV. "I hate that word, 'crossover.' I don't know if it's because it puts too much pressure . . . not really, in a way, but I just don't like that word. There's so many people that have already bought Spanish music in the US. It's just that now it's starting to come out. I just hope this is not like a 'This is one thing that's going to last three months.' I think it won't. I think you'll see it's here to stay."

Even though he didn't need to convince anyone, it seemed that Enrique was trying to confirm the fact that he was much more than just a passing fancy—to the public as well as to himself. While "*Bailamos*" had reached number one on the *Billboard Hot 100*, and helped to lift the *Wild Wild West* soundtrack into the double-platinum bracket, it was hardly Enrique's sole claim to fame. After all, he had devoted his entire life to making music.

Most of all, Enrique resented the pressure. He

knew that the flow of his creativity and imagination could not be rushed, and his inherited perfectionism would not allow him to hurry through the recording process. Nothing had changed since Enrique's first days in the music business, when he'd refused the assistance of his father. The singer still would not let anyone or anything dictate the direction of his music. "I'm in the studio, and I'm experimenting a little bit," explained Enrique. "I'm very hands-on, so I just can't do one of those albums where I just come in, I sing the song, and I leave. I like to write. I like to be in the whole process of the albums. So it's going to take me some time to think of what I want to do, exactly, and what kind of an album I want to do. So it's not that easy."

Easy or not, he wouldn't have it any other way.

Enrique Iglesias's life may seem charmed and privileged to the outside world, but there has never been anything "easy" about the path he has chosen. In fact, Enrique thrives on making things as difficult as possible and overcoming the many odds stacked against him.

From his very first foray into the recording business as Enrique Martinez to his extensive touring and promotional schedule, the young singer was dead-set on escaping the immense shadow of his father's success and his own natural shyness. A single glance at the music charts and his electrifying live performance is all you need to see that Enrique Iglesias is one man who has made all of his dreams come true.

So if you ever bump into him on the street or have a moment to chat while he signs an autograph, don't join the throngs of inquiring reporters who've grilled him on everything from his alleged feud with his father to his choice of wardrobe to his girlfriends. All you need to do is ask, "What does it take to hold on to a dream and never let it go?" and you'll get the one answer that Enrique has worked his whole life to figure out.

TEN

Enrique in Space

Enrique has been around the world and back, so it was only fitting that he should take over space as well—cyberspace that is. Many of his loyal admirers have set up web shrines to pay homage to the almighty deity, and you can join in the fun by simply logging on to the Internet and checking out some of these incredible web pages.

Magazines and newspapers reporting on Enrique's whereabouts are all well and good, but what about those times when you need a fast fix? One article just won't do when you're in the mood to spend hours poring over pictures, talking to like-minded Enrique fans, or downloading some new.wavs. So go ahead and surf on over to one of these preselected sites. You'll be glad you did.

Enrique Official
http://www.enriqueig.com/stage/scripts/rgSplash.asp

You can expect great things from Enrique's official site. He's never let us down before, and wouldn't think of starting now. On this well-designed and easy-to-navigate site, you'll find anything and everything about Enrique. Whether you're interested in finding out about his background, listening to some new sounds, reading great articles, or checking out hot pictures of the Latin singer, you'll find all that and a lot more at this wonderful site.

Final Grade: A+

Enrique Iglesias
http://www.geocities.com/Broadway/3048/ei.html

This is the hands-down winner of the Enrique Iglesias web sites. Karen, the webmaster, is truly one of Enrique's biggest fans. The care and consideration she puts into updating this site is proof that she is one fan who is intent on making Enrique look his absolute best. You'll find everything you'll need, including loads of cool photos taken by the web page creator herself, an active message board, links, news, sounds, and even greeting cards.

Final Grade: A+

Maria's Enrique Iglesias Page
http://members.tripod.com/~EnriqueIglesias/

This doozy of a site boasts a clean layout and a cool look that is bound to stimulate your senses. But all flash and no substance would have made even this looker into a dull page. Not to worry. You'll find plenty of information here. There's a complete list of options, including a picture archive, tour updates, tons of links, a complete biography, and even a discussion forum where you can catch up on all the latest gossip. Stop by and see it for yourself.

Final Grade: A

Priscila's Enrique Iglesias Page
http://www.fortunecity.com/tinpan/suede/737

With both Spanish and English versions available, this site is definitely in keeping with Enrique's bilingual fan base. You'll also discover pictures of the Latin heartthrob himself, an unabridged biography, and a chat room where you can interact with fans from all over the world. With a little more content, this site is sure to become one of the best.

Final Grade: B

Suzie's Cosas de Enrique Site
http://www.cosas-de-enrique.com

This is one site that has everything going for it. From the looks of it alone, it seems as if the webmaster has taken her fair share of HTML courses. An elegant look coupled with tons of great information makes this site a contender for "Best of the Web." With tons of photos, articles, tour info, and lyrics, you are bound to have hours of nonstop entertainment.

Final Grade: A—

The Enrique Iglesias International Fan Club
http://www.enriqueiglesias.com/

The International Fan Club is one place where fans from around the world can unite for the good of one common cause. A bold design and quick-to-load pages also contribute to making this site a must-see on your tour through Enrique's cyber-galaxy. Here you'll find a bevy of facts, pictures, concert dates, challenging quizzes, and a bulletin board where you can post your thoughts or talk about your Enrique concert experiences.

Final Grade: A

Enrique Iglesias Home
http://iglesias.resoftfree.com/

While this site is one of the newest additions to the Internet community, it already has a unique feature that sets it above the rest. The webmaster has been so gracious as to include a total of eight galleries of Enrique photos, complete with a picture from every phase of his career. Topping off this massive collection of pics is a complete discography, a well-written bio, and links to other cool sites. Prepare to stay awhile.

Final Grade: B+

About the Authors

Elina and Leah Furman are the authors of numerous celebrity biographies such as *Ricky Martin, James Van Der Beek, The Heat Is On: 98 Degrees, Give It to You: The Jordan Knight Story,* and *Heart of Soul: The Lauryn Hill Story.* Some of their other titles include *The Everything After College Book, Generation Inc.,* and *The Everything Dating Book.*

Meet Hollywood's Coolest Young Superstar!

MATT DAMON

By Kathleen Tracy

Matt Damon is more than just a handsome heartthrob—he's also a talented actor and screenwriter who took home both a Golden Globe Award and an Oscar for co-writing the movie *Good Will Hunting*. Find out how he made it in Hollywood, what he plans for the future, about his lifelong friendship with Ben Affleck, about his steamy relationships with some of his leading ladies, and much, much more! Includes eight pages of exciting photos.

MATT DAMON
Kathleen Tracy
0-312-96857-4 _____ $4.99 U.S. _____ $6.50 CAN.

Publishers Book and Audio Mailing Service
P.O. Box 070059, Staten Island, NY 10307
Please send me the book(s) I have checked above. I am enclosing $_____ (please add $1.50 for the first book, and $.50 for each additional book to cover postage and handling. Send check or money order only—no CODs) or charge my VISA, MASTERCARD, DISCOVER or AMERICAN EXPRESS card.

Card Number_____

Expiration date_____Signature_____

Name_____

Address_____

City_____State/Zip_____
Please allow six weeks for delivery. Prices subject to change without notice. Payment in U.S. funds only. New York residents add applicable sales tax.

DAMON 10/98

GET THE 411 ON YOUR FAVORITE SINGERS!

B*WITCHED
0-312-97360-8___$4.99___$6.50 Can.

BACKSTREET BOYS
0-312-96853-1___$3.99___$4.99 Can.

BRANDY
0-312-97055-2___$4.99___$6.50 Can.

FIVE
0-312-97225-3___$4.99___$6.50 Can.

LAURYN HILL
0-312-97210-5___$5.99___$7.99 Can.

RICKY MARTIN
0-312-97322-5___$4.99___$6.50 Can.

THE MOFFATTS
0-312-97359-4___$4.99___$6.50 Can.

98°
0-312-97200-8___$4.99___$6.50 Can.

N SYNC
0-312-97198-2___$4.99___$6.50 Can.

BRITNEY SPEARS
0-312-97268-7___$4.99___$6.50 Can.

Publishers Book and Audio Mailing Service
P.O. Box 070059, Staten Island, NY 10307
Please send me the book(s) I have checked above. I am enclosing $_____ (please add
$1.50 for the first book, and $.50 for each additional book to cover postage and handling.
Send check or money order only—no CODs) or charge my VISA, MASTERCARD,
DISCOVER or AMERICAN EXPRESS card.

Card Number_____

Expiration date_____Signature_____

Name_____

Address_____

City_____State/Zip_____
Please allow six weeks for delivery. Prices subject to change without notice. Payment in
U.S. funds only. New York residents add applicable sales tax.   celeb6/99

GET THE SIZZLING INSIDE
STORY ON THE WORLD'S
HOTTEST BAND!

BACKSTREET BOYS

They've Got it Goin' On!

Anna Louise Golden

**Find out all about AJ, Brian, Howie,
Kevin, and Nick—step into their world,
see what makes them tick, what kind of
girls they like, how they make their
way-cool music, and much, much more!
Includes eight pages of cool color photos.**

BACKSTREET BOYS
Anna Louise Golden
0-312-96853-1_____ $3.99 U.S. _____ $4.99 CAN.

Publishers Book and Audio Mailing Service
P.O. Box 070059, Staten Island, NY 10307
Please send me the book(s) I have checked above. I am enclosing $_____ (please add
$1.50 for the first book, and $.50 for each additional book to cover postage and handling.
Send check or money order only—no CODs) or charge my VISA, MASTERCARD,
DISCOVER or AMERICAN EXPRESS card.

Card Number_____

Expiration date_____Signature_____

Name_____

Address_____

City_____State/Zip _____
Please allow six weeks for delivery. Prices subject to change without notice. Payment in
U.S. funds only. New York residents add applicable sales tax.

BOYS 10/98

GET ALL THE COOL FACTS ON YOUR FAVORITE CELEBS!

MATT DAMON
0-312-96857-4___$4.99___$6.50 Can.

SALMA HAYEK
0-312-96982-1___$4.99___$6.50 Can.

JENNIFER LOPEZ
0-312-97085-4___$4.99___$6.50 Can.

JENNIFER LOVE HEWITT
0-312-96991-0___$4.99___$6.50 Can.

EWAN McGREGOR
0-312-96910-4___$5.99___$7.99 Can.

WILL SMITH
0-312-96722-5___$4.99___$6.50 Can.

JAMES VAN DER BEEK
0-312-97226-1___$5.99___$7.99 Can.

Publishers Book and Audio Mailing Service
P.O. Box 070059, Staten Island, NY 10307
Please send me the book(s) I have checked above. I am enclosing $_____ (please add
$1.50 for the first book, and $.50 for each additional book to cover postage and handling.
Send check or money order only—no CODs) or charge my VISA, MASTERCARD,
DISCOVER or AMERICAN EXPRESS card.

Card Number_____

Expiration date_____Signature_____

Name_____

Address_____

City_____State/Zip _____
    Please allow six weeks for delivery. Prices subject to change without notice. Payment in
U.S. funds only. New York residents add applicable sales tax.   celeb.8/99

Get the sizzling inside story on the hot
young star of song and screen

SITTIN' ON TOP OF THE WORLD
ANNA LOUISE GOLDEN

Named one of the "21 hottest stars under 21" by *Teen
People* magazine, Brandy, the chart-topping singer and
star of TV's *Moesha*, is one of today's hottest young
talents—a bright, headstrong woman who handles the
hurdles of stardom with major maturity, while enjoy-
ing life like an ordinary teenager (she talks for hours
on the phone, shops up a storm, and *loves* McDonald's
french fries!). Get the 411 on this award-winning
superstar and her life in front of the camera, in back of
the microphone—and *behind* the scenes.

WITH EIGHT PAGES OF FABULOUS PHOTOS!

BRANDY
Anna Louise Golden
0-312-97055-2___$4.99 U.S.___$6.50 Can.

Publishers Book and Audio Mailing Service
P.O. Box 070059, Staten Island, NY 10307
Please send me the book(s) I have checked above. I am enclosing $_____ (please add
$1.50 for the first book, and $.50 for each additional book to cover postage and handling.
Send check or money order only—no CODs) or charge my VISA, MASTERCARD,
DISCOVER or AMERICAN EXPRESS card.

Card Number_____

Expiration date_____Signature_____

Name_____

Address_____

City_____State/Zip _____
Please allow six weeks for delivery. Prices subject to change without notice. Payment in
U.S. funds only. New York residents add applicable sales tax.   BRANDY 3/99